The Wadsworth Series in Composition Studies

Collaborative Writing in Composition Studies

Sheryl I. Fontaine

California State University, Fullerton

Susan M. Hunter

Kennesaw State University

THOMSON

™

WADSWORTH

Australia • Canada • Mexico • Singapore • Spain
United Kingdom • United States

Publisher: *Michael Rosenberg*
Acquisitions Editor: *Dickson Musslewhite*
Editorial Assistant: *Dawn Giovanniello*
Marketing Manager: *Carrie Brandon*
Advertising Project Manager: *Brian Chaffee*

Editorial Production Manager: *Michael Burggren*
Manufacturing Supervisor: *Marcia Locke*
Cover Designer: *Dutton & Sherman Design*
Production Service/Compositor: *Integra*
Cover/Text Printer: *Webcom Limited*

Printed in Canada
1 2 3 4 5 6 7 08 07 06 05 04

For more information about our products, contact us at:
Thomson Learning Academic Resource Center
1-800-423-0563

For permission to use material from this text or product, submit a request online at
http://www.thomsonrights.com.
Any additional questions about permissions can be submitted by email to
thomsonrights@thomson.com.

Thomson Higher Education
25 Thomson Place
Boston, MA 02210-1202
USA

Asia (including India)
Thomson Learning
5 Shenton Way
#01-01 UIC Building
Singapore 068808

Australia/New Zealand
Thomson Learning Australia
102 Dodds Street
Southbank, Victoria 3006
Australia

Canada
Thomson Nelson
1120 Birchmount Road
Toronto, Ontario M1K 5G4
Canada

UK/Europe/Middle East/Africa
Thomson Learning
High Holborn House
50/51 Bedford Row
London WC1R 4LR
United Kingdom

Library of Congress Control Number:
2004098268

ISBN 0-155-06968-3

Contents

The Wadsworth Series in Composition Studies may be the first book series intended specifically for an audience of advanced undergraduate and beginning graduate students who are studying the discipline of Composition. Until now, faculty have been left to assign to their students collections or articles that were originally written for experts in the field and, consequently, assume a level of expert knowledge of the field and awareness of scholars and theories that these students are unlikely to possess. The Wadsworth Series in Composition Studies provides instructors a distinct alternative to using collections, one that is both appropriate and inviting for this less experienced but professionally directed audience. Each book in the series introduces the discipline by examining one aspect of the work in which Composition specialists engage. Providing practical information, the books also present students relevant theoretical underpinnings from within the discipline, using terminology and historical explanations that beginning students in the field need and can understand.

As series editors, we believe that once invited into Composition Studies by means of the books in this series, students will be better able to enact the field for themselves, for graduate student peers, and for future colleagues in English studies. Moreover, using these books, all students will carry away with them a truer picture of what Composition specialists do, how we think, and what we care about in our classrooms and our research.

Sheryl I. Fontaine
Susan M. Hunter
Series Editors

Preface for the Instructor

Meeting the Need for a New Instructional Genre with The Wadsworth Series in Composition Studies[1]

Why Do We Need a New Genre?

Because this is the inaugural book in a new series of a new instructional genre, we want to explain the motivation behind the concept. We hope that our explanation will give you, the instructor, an even better sense of how this book, and others from the series, can be used to provide your students with a fundamental understanding of Composition Studies, how it might be integrated into your classes. Our decision to coauthor a book on collaborative writing that we could use in our courses, a book that our students would understand, emerged from our own dissatisfaction with available texts. As all of us who teach upper division and graduate-level courses in Composition know from our own experiences, there are very few textbooks written exclusively for our students. In fact, the idea of a *textbook* for students at this level is hard for many of us to imagine. Instead, students are expected to read the same journals and books that we order for ourselves.

Now, consider this reading list in light of the fact that most of our students have chosen to study in the field, not because they have had introductory courses in the history of Composition or the kinds of questions the discipline asks, but because they are interested in issues related to the process of writing, rhetoric, or the teaching of writing. In some instances, they are required to take a course in Composition and Rhetoric.

---

[1] A version of this preface was presented at the Conference on College Composition and Communication in New York in March 2003, and another version appears in *Culture Shock: Training the New Wave in Rhetoric and Composition.* Ed. Virginia Anderson and Susan Romano. Cresskill, NJ: Hampton Press, Inc., 2004.

And given that we have little choice but to assign collections or articles that were originally written for experts who already have a foundational awareness of scholars and knowledge in the field, our students find themselves thrown mid-stream into discussions that are ongoing, already in progress. Our students generally have no disciplinary background from which to enter this 40-year-long contemporary conversation, let alone the ancient conversations from which the discipline emerged thousands of years ago. In an attempt to help their understanding, we scramble to provide basic historical and theoretical background, interpret the jargon, explicate the unfamiliar references, and hope that students won't become disillusioned or discouraged by what they had expected to be an eminently practical discipline.

Composition is a maturing (if not mature) discipline. Certainly the challenges we all have experienced teaching to an ever-increasing number of students in our discipline-based courses with the available texts has made clear the pedagogical difficulties of using texts written for experts to teach classrooms of novices. Why, then, we wondered has the emergence of texts written specifically for these courses and their students been so very slow to happen? One important answer to this question has to do with the instructional models that dominate our classrooms and that, in fact, promote what we would identify as an awkward use or even a misuse of texts. Indeed, if teachers had access to appropriately targeted texts, they would not only find their students more adequately grounded in the discipline, they might also be more free to move away from the familiar mode of instruction that has been inherited. In other words, rather than creating curricula structured around readings and exercises intended to replicate expert knowledge, we might draw on a new genre of texts written for upper division students to design a curriculum whose rhythms draw on habits of mind characteristic of Composition teachers, administrators, and researchers. The genre we propose encourages faculty to design graduate curricula in Composition that would include accessible and invitational introductions to ways of thinking and practicing in the field. If this genre of text were available as preliminary or alternative to the collections of professional articles and academic research tomes currently available for adoption in upper level undergraduate and graduate courses, these texts written expressly to be instructional and invitational would doubtless stimulate new ways of thinking about teaching the field.

What Is the Predominant Instructional Approach?

Perhaps the most familiar and longest lasting instructional approach for bringing students into the academy is by way of immersing them into the discipline (see Berkenkotter, Huckin, and Ackerman; North et al.). As we conceive it, this approach assumes that the best way to bring students into a discipline is by lowering them directly into its professional literature. Students are expected to jump directly into the middle of expert-level discussions and, through a sink-or-swim process, come to understand the various arguments and their relation to one another, thereby achieving advanced literacy in the field. Let's consider some of the research that illustrates the use and effects of this approach.

In their research on graduate student writing, Carol Berkenkotter, Thomas Huckin, and John Ackerman demonstrate disciplinary immersion or indoctrination in their case study of what they call the "cognitive apprenticeship" of a student named "Nate." Nate struggles to make the transition from informal prose to academic discourse within a disciplinary community, to assimilate the linguistic style, the academic register, and the genre conventions of the Rhetoric Program at Carnegie Mellon in the mid-1980s (see "Social Context and Socially Constructed Texts" and *Genre Knowledge* 116–44). According to the researchers, this case study shows how "Students begin as novices, or newcomers to the community and begin their enculturation through peripheral forms of participation that change over time as apprentices change their status from newcomers to members" (118). Noting Nate's background as a writing teacher and a writer with a "literary, journalistic prose style," Berkenkotter, Huckin, and Ackerman analyze the "linguistic and rhetorical features that are discrepant with the discourse conventions of social science expository prose that [Nate] will be expected to use later at Carnegie Mellon" (121). What this admittedly "skilled adult writer" brought to the program with him from his prior professional life, then, was deemed "discrepant," different and without value in this unfamiliar context. Consequently, by means of immersion, his prior skills need to be unlearned and replaced with the preferred modes of the researchers in the discourse community he was trying to enter. In other words, succumbing to instructional immersion in order to become academically literate, Nate has to embrace the formal discourse of expertise and has to reject what Cheryl Geisler identifies as indigenous modes of discourse (89–91).

Building on this research and writing from the perspective of an editorial board member of a professional journal in Composition Studies,

Richard McNabb claims that this immersion in disciplinary knowledge is necessary for students to become publishing scholars, insiders within the community's discourse. He construes the kind of "gesturing" students will learn from the immersion approach as an ability "to shift authority away from everyday professional practices, that is, the material sites of one's activities—classrooms, department hallways, conferences—and into a structured realm of epistemological and methodological frameworks" (11). Scholars like these we have named as well as many others expect students to renounce personal register, "indigenous culture," and resituate themselves in order to become insiders who can authorize and make knowledge in Composition Studies.

Such an approach to instruction promotes what Stephen M. North in *Refiguring the Ph.D. in English Studies* has identified as the "magisterial," "professor-as-master" relationship between faculty and student (29). Being immersed directly into the kind of literature they are expected eventually to (re)produce, students can be encouraged to write "about" topics that easily emerge from the professional readings and comfortably fit within the topics of the course syllabus. According to North, students'

> writings [are] also supposed to (re)present one or another similarly sanctioned method of inquiry, not only in terms of deploying various evidentiary systems, but also in a more overtly behavioral sense, wherein textual conventions are assumed to regulate (or at least to signify the regulation of) the students' investigative activities. Indeed, the ideal outcome in this approach is for the apprentice to produce a text that could plausibly have been written by the master. (129)

A 2001 *CCC* Interchanges among members of a Dissertation Consortium focused on reimagining the dissertation in composition and rhetoric further illustrates the continuing impact of the magisterial position that North describes. One discussant attests to the fact that in her role as dissertation advisor her attempts to foster

> innovation, revision, and change in relation to the dissertation in particular and academic writing in general [. . .] [are] met with a conversation-stopping assertion of responsibility: "I have a responsibility to teach my students the conventions"; "I'm responsible for ensuring that my doctoral students write a solid, get-a-job dissertation"; "It's my responsibility to show I really know the field, really know my stuff". (443)

In these words we hear a particular sense of what it means to be a "responsible" teacher, one for whom replication is the imperative; immersion the way to foster it.

What Are the Limitations of the Immersion Approach?

However, the very fact that this Interchange was published in a major disciplinary journal and that not all of its members shared the views cited above suggests the discipline's willingness to question the master–apprentice relationship and the prevailing professional identity that the immersion/magisterial approach/curriculum authorizes. Notably using the metaphor of a bridge rather than immersion, another member of the Dissertation Consortium makes an appeal for a very different, more respectably balanced instructor–student relationship: He perceives "the force of what graduate students do not know bridging them into what they are beginning to know, the force of what professors know bridging them into what they do not know" (452). This appeal reminds us of North's own call for a curriculum that assumes students can and should be participants rather than imitators.

To see how the immersion approach has particular limitations for students of Composition Studies, let's first consider the situation of literature students. By the time they reach their final year of university or have entered a graduate program, they have been reading and studying the primary and secondary key texts of the discipline for many years. "Immersing" these students is, more accurately, a re-immersion or an extended immersion in a discipline they began visiting years ago. In contrast, upper division undergraduate and graduate students in Composition are in a very different position when they enter our classrooms. And as one of us has noted elsewhere,

> Except for students at those very few schools that offer one or two undergraduate courses in composition [. . .] undergraduates get, at most, a casual sense of the discipline from the one or two specialists in the department, freshman composition instructors who off-handedly refer to the discipline, graduate student hearsay, or the limited experience available to undergraduates as peer tutors in a writing center. (Fontaine 327)

So, having had little, if any, introduction to the history of Composition or the kinds of questions the discipline asks, as we said earlier, these students may have chosen this field because they are interested in issues related to the process of writing, rhetoric, or the teaching of writing. They may have accidentally discovered our composition courses or graduate programs when they were perusing the department's offerings. However they got there, we can expect that many of them have no disciplinary background from which to enter the contemporary conversations of the discipline or even the ancient conversations from which it emerged. The possibility of "immersing" these minimally experienced students into all of the disciplinary literature along with the concepts and ways of thinking of our discipline during one or two introductory courses is impossible. And as Composition becomes increasingly complex, it becomes even more difficult to imagine individual courses or instructors providing students with comprehensive overviews or introductions to the field. Our best remedy is to assign essays originally written for an audience of experts and professionals and rely on these to inform students, taking time from our seminars, when necessary, to provide students with as much basic historical and theoretical background as time permits. Needless to say, the breadth of this background is limited, and because of the multiple and distinct areas of specialization within Composition, such overviews are necessarily abridged, often delivered through the perspective of our own interests and expertise.

So, even if we wanted to accept an immersion approach, its feasibility for our students decreases each year. Yet, anthologies of previously published journal articles that promote immersion proliferate, and the market for these collections is the instructor of the teaching practicum and graduate courses in composition and rhetoric.

Little research has been done to determine how effectively our curricula introduce students into the discipline. In fact, as we have already noted, the most recent research done on graduate students' entry into the discipline has largely focused on their learning how to produce academic texts rather than on their learning how to read in the field. However, looking at our own experiences with students in upper division and graduate-level courses on writing pedagogy, writing process, tutoring pedagogy, and so forth, we can see the results of teaching with an immersion approach. As we have suggested, the readings in most of the courses we teach for upper division undergraduate or entering graduate students include articles from recent issues of *College Composition and Communication, Research in the Teaching of English,* and *College English,* or from edited collections of these or similar essays. It is common, particularly early in the semester, for students to be confused and even overwhelmed when we assign these readings. For example, in an introductory course on issues and research in a master's program, students typically accuse the authors of assigned articles or book excerpts of being "bad" writers because they allude to a lot of experts and cite texts that the students have never heard of. Acting like the laypersons or the general public that Geisler identifies, they reject "academic prose" and its "gestures" as elitist, as somehow "denying legitimacy to their everyday knowledge" (80). And, to a large extent, they are right to do so, even if they are naïve in their representation of the texts in question. Resisting immersion, students give up quite easily on such articles and, consequently, may dismiss the field of Composition entirely. Seminars can become disjointed, and because they are put off by the apparent jargon and unfamiliar litany of references, students become frustrated by the theoretical and academic nature of what they expected to be a practical discipline.

Carl Bereiter and Marlene Scardamalia's research on the nature of expertise may give us a way to understand why the immersion approach as the sole introduction to Composition Studies doesn't work and why students may be put off by articles and essays from our professional publications. Without prior knowledge of Composition, novices like our students may rely on direct assimilation, matching new information to old knowledge, to acquire new knowledge. They behave as inexpert learners when they come across new information in the texts we ask them to read, "find[ing] the best fit and go[ing] with it even if the fit is not very good" (169). In doing so, the students have "settled on some interpretation that is likely to stand in the way of further learning" (169). Like the "nonexpert learners" described by Bereiter and Scarmadalia, our students often "jump to conclusions on the basis of the little they have already learned." They "make subjective judgments of importance." They "assume words mean what they are used to having them mean." They tend to "construct simplistic interpretations, which are then retained in the face of contraindications." They "often dismiss whole topics as boring, without attempting to discover what might be interesting in them, while allowing themselves to be captivated by items of tangential interest" (170).

It is the expert approach to the study of a field that is entirely new to them—constructing a knowledge-building schema—that our students need to be invited to learn. With this approach, according to Bereiter and Scardamalia, they would realize that "there is probably more to be learned than [they] can imagine at the outset." They are "unable to tell what is important from what isn't, and so [they] had better err on the side of assuming things are important." They would be alert to the fact that "words that [they] think [they] already know may turn out to have different meanings in the new discipline" and that initially their "understanding is likely to be simplistic, and so [they] had better be on the watch for complicating factors." Finally, they would realize that "no matter how unappealing the field might at first seem to [them], there are intelligent people who find it fascinating, and so [they] should be on the watch for what it is that arouses the intellectual passions of people in the new discipline" (169–70).

By not immersing students into the expert discourse of the field when they are still novices, the contextualized curricula that we are encouraging through the introduction of a new instructional genre acknowledges students' position at the threshold of disciplinary knowledge and prepares them to become expert learners in the field of Composition. As we will explain, this instructional genre supports the classroom as a "knowledge-building community" where knowledge is shared and members "support one another in knowledge construction, and they develop a kind of collective expertise that is distinguishable from that of the individual [student]" (202). As an introduction to the discipline different from that issued by an immersion approach, this new genre pre-figures for newcomers to the academic field of Composition the way that "progressive knowledge-building discourse" works in the disciplinary community they are trying to enter.

What Alternative Instructional Approaches Are Emerging?

Graduate programs that rely on immersing fledgling composition students into the professional literature of the discipline, then, are problematic on several levels. First, unlike many other disciplines, ours seldom appears as a subject of study in lower division curricula; students in our upper division undergraduate and graduate student classes commonly have very little if any background in composition and rhetoric. So not only is such an approach truly a full baptismal immersion for students, it submerges them in the rough-running stream of the discipline.

This approach is problematic also because, as we have suggested, the essays, articles, and books that students are immersed in were most likely not written for this novice, uninformed reader. Because their authors assumed their readers would have knowledge of the debates, research, and conceptual developments out of which the authors are writing, the texts tend to leave students confused about or even resentful of obscure textual allusions, unfamiliar references, and expectations that they participate in a completely foreign conversation.

And finally, the curricula which support this approach to instruction are often designed so as to mirror the descriptive categories into which the texts themselves were originally placed. That is, the journals or essay collections are easily sorted by their titles or their contents into the kinds of "archival" categories that Geisler attributes to "acquisitions editors who perceive a market in a specific area" (33) and that we, consequently, see listed in book catalogues and lining shelves in bookstores or libraries: "research," "pedagogy," "writing across the disciplines," "theory," or similar topic areas that are repeated in course titles and areas of study. Given that such naming of categories shapes the discipline as well as the perceptions about the discipline (Armstrong and Fontaine), our novice students begin their study of the discipline with a false sense that its members can and do work in single areas of study—the researcher does not tread into the subject area of the pedagogue who, similarly, avoids the territory of the theorist; we are teachers or researchers or theory formulators, but not all three or even more than one at a time.

If one of our goals for students, particularly those students who are unfamiliar with Composition Studies, is to welcome them in a manner that is appropriate to their level of experience, expertise, and interest, then we would do well to consider the "power of invitation" that Mike Rose celebrates in his discussion of underprepared students (132). This particular invitation does not assume that students are already comfortable and familiar with the material, nor does it attempt to present an entire body of material in one sweeping gesture. Rather, by opening the door for students, letting them enter the academic conversation with the kind of support and encouragement that is needed when one enters a foreign territory, the invitation serves as a beginning from which the rest of the journey is made. Speaking less metaphorically, and in terms of our own "underprepared" Composition students, we might think about the invitation we offer them when they begin our graduate programs. For whether or not these students major in Composition Studies or select it as a field for graduate study and how they will engage in the work of the discipline once selected depends, in large part, on how they first perceive and experience the field and its research.

As we consider approaches to instruction and design of upper division and graduate curricula, we should critically ask ourselves how often the emphasis of the training "and the professorial commitment that follows from it are toward the preservation of the discipline, not the intellectual development of young people" (Rose 197). Certainly it appears that, when considered together, a topics'-based curricular design, the familiar immersion approach to instruction, and the magisterial position taken by faculty are predicated on the idea that students' goal is to reproduce the work of the master and, in that sense, preserve the discipline. But long before students take on or try out the professional identity of a publishing scholar, they have to understand what the field is about and be attracted enough to its questions and methods to take on the challenge of reading the scholarship of the field. That is to say, in order to make an appropriately founded choice about studying Composition or to develop a valid sense of what the discipline is, students need to understand the way Composition specialists "see," to anticipate the kinds of questions they ask, and to appreciate the value of the answers.

Furthermore, students who enter the discipline by means of this instructional approach—alongside of or in place of the immersion approach—will begin their professional lives with a clearer, better prepared sense of its ways of seeing and thinking. Given that Composition becomes increasingly complex in its structure—no longer easily separated into categories of teaching, research, and theory—the kind of instructional genre in this series should decrease the amount of time that new assistant professors spend floundering in the transition between graduate school and employment—a floundering that, we believe, is caused, not only by the inevitable position-transition, but by the way in which our graduate programs misrepresent the activity of the field. New faculty are left on their own to shift from seeing the discipline through a series of library catalogue categories, to seeing it as an integrated, systematic way of thinking. Such instruction will, in turn, enrich the profession by providing a graduate training program that truly reflects the discipline and, moreover, will help the next generation of scholars who will be ensconced in a more fully integrated apprenticeship.

Indeed, recently proposed revisions to the Composition curriculum reflect a shift from studying and replicating representative "topics" to experiencing the behaviors and practices of the discipline. Consider the alternatives proposed by Richard Fulkerson, Robert Scholes, and Stephen M. North, each of which, to a different degree, presumes that the discipline should be studied in terms of its professional behaviors or ways of thinking about problems.

Fulkerson would like to extend a fairly traditional graduate curriculum of theory and practice to include a "metacurriculum" that "appropriate[s] apprenticeship experience not just of scholarship, but for the full life of being a professor [...]" (130). So while the first two-thirds of the curriculum represents the rather expected division of theory/practice, this split would be extended into a triad that includes courses like the study of pedagogy, the philosophy of education, the sociology of the profession, the politics of the profession, and educational and professional history (131). While other writers (e.g. see Pemberton) have argued the value of focusing students' attention on the roles they will hold in the profession that are like the ones we, as their senior mentors, already hold, Fulkerson pushes his goals for the metacurriculum further. It is intended *not* to prepare students for reproducing the work of the master, but, rather, to teach them about the culture into which they are entering: what constitutes the premises on which it was built, what determines its standards and values, and how to identify and maneuver around its hazards.

Moving a bit further from the traditional topics/immersion approach, Scholes in *The Rise and Fall of English* proposes a "modern trivium" that is "organized around a canon of concepts, precepts, and practices rather than a canon of texts" (120) that is to be understood not just in a theoretical way, but in terms of its "application to the analysis of specific cultural or textual objects" (121). Throughout the description of his "trivium," Scholes suggests that rather than be expected to examine and replicate a canon of texts, students will be taught to consider each individual concept and practice of the discipline as an "activity," (122) or "process" (123) by which one generates a view of the world, one that makes "available to students the tradition of clear and systematic thinking" (125). Moreover, rather than focusing on "immersing students" in texts so they will internalize and imitate the language and subject matter of the master, the goal of this course of study is to "encourage textual production [...] in appropriate modes" (120). In the case of Composition, then, students are more likely to acquire the perspective, processes, and behaviors that the Composition specialist relies on to make sense of the world, if they enter the discipline via its concepts, precepts, and practices.

And finally, North focuses entirely on developing students' disciplinary position. This is done by introducing students to "seven interrelated branches of study" (90), that are "understood as marking points of entry, places from which to *enter* that inquiry-in-progress that is the discipline" of Composition (91). Furthermore, North identifies this introduction for students as an "integrative approach" that presents a "coordinated series of occasions for negotiating claims about who knows what, how, why, and to what ends" (92). Like Scholes, North uses writing as a means by which students can begin to experience and adopt the language and enter the conversation of the discipline. However, while Scholes promotes a somewhat ambiguous use of "appropriate modes," North's proposal is clearer and broader, suggesting students will be provided with the information and strategies that allow them to identify points of entry into the conversation of the discipline and methods of inquiry they can use once an entrance is found.

What Features Make This New Genre of Text Distinctive?

While the curricular proposals made by Fulkerson, Scholes, and North certainly have identifying differences, they share an approach to textual study that at least extends and at most replaces the immersion approach. But if, as we and others argue, there is a need to teach students by means other than submersion into texts written for Composition experts and categorized by archival-type topics, then there is a commensurate need for an alternative textual genre through which to "teach" the discipline. The one we put forward in this series does not presume to serve up archival information in the decontextualized manner of annotated bibliography, bibliographic essay, or literature review. Rather this genre is written specifically for the novice, student audience; contains terminology and explanations appropriate to beginning students in the field; reads in a voice whose real, immediate quality extends an invitation to the reader; presents as its objects of study the behaviors and ways of thought significant to and identifying of the discipline; and, consequently, "introduces" students to the history, theories, writers, and researchers of Composition Studies by means of these behaviors. Such a genre reflects curricula whose rhythms draw on habits of the mind much more than the replication of expert knowledge. Concepts like social constructionism, authorship, or interpretive communities and practices such as dialogue journals, peer response, or focused freewriting appear in the context of the professional occasions or particular intellectual challenges in which they are important. Rather than texts whose topics echo course titles—"Research in Composition," "Teaching Basic Writing"—and whose chapters become the headings for the weeks of a semester-long course, this new genre of text presents theoretical or practical concepts and methods of inquiry that could cross courses. Consequently, students are provided with what North calls "*the* central disciplining activity," one that teaches "graduate students to situate themselves properly with respect to whatever are imagined to be, in a given time and place, the discipline's key texts" (110).

We are reminded again of the novice/expert research that claims "… novice learning is contingent on concept formation and assimilation. Novice learning is also framed by the feelings novices experience in the context of practice" (Daley 133). The new textual genre we are describing not only provides a scaffold of concepts to frame and support the discipline, it engages the student in practical activities and heuristics—response papers, written dialogue, interviews—within which to assimilate the concepts and move beyond a "threshold position" of study (North 114). That is, the goal of this new genre of text, when placed into our curriculum, is to get students reading and writing in the conventions of the discipline (beyond its threshold) without losing something of the students' individuality or the complexity of the discipline on the journey. The immersion approach, particularly when transmitted from a "magisterial" professor, risks limiting the thinking and independent conceptualization processes of student writers who are being encouraged to imitate and reproduce the ideas and language into which they are being submerged. The alternative genre of this series, because it focuses on disciplinary habits of mind, concepts, and practices, promotes a larger kind of thinking where the limits are not set by the ideological shadows of the professional literature, but by the less ominous, though equally demanding parameters of culture and convention.

As we have suggested, the texts we are envisioning are designed to contextualize the theory, history, and practice of the field within the particular subjects of study and practice that are unique to specialists in our discipline. Each one introduces the discipline by examining one particular kind of work in which Composition specialists engage. And although the texts provide practical information, they also present students with related theoretical underpinnings of this practice, contextualizing the practice in the discipline using terminology and historical explanations that beginning students in the field need and can understand.

To make this concept more concrete, let's use this book, *Collaborative Writing in Composition Studies*, as an example. For some time now, Composition scholars have agreed that collaborative writing is a respected process that achieves valuable results for both writers and readers. They have promoted the distinctive characteristics of the collaborative process and collaborative writing, its importance to the profession, and the need for all students to be prepared to write with others. However, in spite of its value across the profession, collaborative writing is not usually a subject of study in our graduate programs. In order to appreciate collaborative writing as a distinct creative behavior, a way of thinking, and a mode of inquiry for the discipline, we believe that graduate students must be able to untangle the complexities of the process of writing together.

As a concept and behavior, collaborative writing easily intersects with discussions you might have with your students on teaching, language development, professional politics, or research, providing both an interface among these issues and a plethora of theoretical, historical, practical touchstones for the novice readers in your classes. Into our text on collaborative writing, then, we have integrated historical information about changing views of knowledge, theoretical information about the social and dialogic nature of language, and practical information about promotion and tenure processes and how to make successful collaborative writing happen. Our text, and the others in the series, cannot be pigeon-holed for courses on research or teaching. Rather, it provides the kind of "integrated" approach to an issue that is reflective of a more integrated, conceptually-based curriculum.

While we have found that many colleagues agree with us about the need for books that will be useful in a classroom of students new to Composition Studies, we have also found that the newness of the genre requires that we guide prospective authors. To do so, we have developed focusing questions and a series template. We suggest that writers ask themselves: What are the behaviors and ways of thinking and seeing that are distinctive to our daily professional lives? How might we present our discipline so as to best imitate such activity and, at the same time, provide students with a clear sense of the complexity of what we do? The following template is intended to identify for authors the desired voice and apparatus that all books in the series share. *The Wadsworth Series in Composition Studies* features:

- New work written specifically for the series.
- An inviting, student-friendly voice that is made alive through the use of new or existing interviews, student voices, voices of colleagues in the field, or other devices that similarly lend a "real," immediate quality to the writing.
- An introduction that makes an overarching connection between the topic of the book and Composition Studies.
- Descriptive headings throughout each chapter.
- Activities such as journal entry topics, questions for consideration, group discussion topics, and informal, reflective writing prompts in each chapter that encourage students to apply the ideas they have read.
- A works cited list at the end of each chapter.
- A list of works For Further Reading concluding each chapter.

How Will This New Genre Affect Future Training in Composition Studies?

Not only will texts like these supply a sort of introduction for our students that is bound to make their transition to disciplinary reading smoother. The advantages accruing to such an approach extend far beyond reduced frustration for master's and doctoral students in Composition as they are introduced to the field. If students are invited into Composition Studies in the way we describe, they will be better able to enact the field for their graduate student peers and future colleagues in English studies.

The future of our discipline and of graduate students' lives as participating members of the discipline will be centrally affected by how well our curricula and texts encourage the kind of integrated reflection and writing that advances a discipline. While it is important for students to understand the conventions of the published discourse, such imitative knowledge risks stalling the progress of the discipline. Rather than asking students to "[enter] the conversation of [our] writing research community by acquiring genre knowledge" and cognitive and rhetorical moves (Berkenkotter, Huckin, and Ackerman 199), we propose inviting them into the profession by means of the professional questions and ways of knowing—the contexts—in which such genre knowledge occurs, an approach which will introduce students to a field that is new to most of them, in a way that encourages the kind of integrative and speculative thinking that makes published discourse more than just a set of repeated conventions. Finally, we are calling for a curricular reform into which such a genre will fit, one that will complement the complexity of our courses and our discipline and that will, in the end, prepare our students for their own original research and for establishing their own personal and professional positions in the discipline.

Works Cited

Armstrong, Cherryl, and Sheryl I. Fontaine. "The Power of Naming: Names that Create and Define the Discipline." *Writing Program Administration* 13 (1989): 5–14.

Bereiter, Carl, and Marlene Scardamalia. *Surpassing Ourselves: An Inquiry into the Nature and Implications of Expertise.* Chicago: Open Court Publishing, 1993.

Berkenkotter, Carol, Thomas N. Huckin, and John Ackerman. "Social Context and Socially Constructed Texts: The Initiation of a Graduate Student into a Writing Research Community." *Textual Dynamics of the Professions: Historical and Contemporary Studies of Writing in Professional Communities.* Ed. Charles Bazerman, and James Paradis. Madison: U of Wisconsin P, 1991. 191–215.

———. *Genre Knowledge in Disciplinary Communication: Cognition/Culture/ Power.* Hillsdale, NJ: Lawrence Erlbaum, 1995. 117–44.

Daley, Barbara J. "Novice to Expert: An Exploration of How Professionals Learn." *Adult Education Quarterly* 49.4 (Summer 1999): 133–48.

The Dissertation Consortium. "Challenging Tradition: A Conversation about Reimagining the Dissertation in Rhetoric and Composition." *College Composition and Communication* 52.3 (February 2001): 441–54.

Fontaine, Sheryl I. "Resuscitating a Terminal Degree: A Reconceptualization of the M.A. in Composition." Fontaine and Hunter. *Writing Ourselves into the Story.* 322–34.

Fontaine, Sheryl I., and Susan M. Hunter. *Collaborative Writing in Composition Studies.* Boston, MA: Wadsworth, 2006.

Fontaine, Sheryl I., and Susan M. Hunter. *Writing Ourselves into the Story: Unheard Voices from Composition Studies.* Carbondale: Southern Illinois UP, 1993.

Fulkerson, Richard. "The English Doctoral Metacurriculum: An Issue of Ethics." *Foregrounding Ethical Awareness in Composition and English Studies.* Ed. Sheryl I. Fontaine and Susan M. Hunter. Portsmouth, NH: Boynton/Cook, 1998. 121–43.

Geisler, Cheryl. *Academic Literacy and the Nature of Expertise: Reading, Writing, and Knowing in Academic Philosophy.* Hillsdale, NJ: Lawrence Erlbaum, 1994.

McNabb, Richard. "Making the Gesture: Graduate Student Submissions and the Expectation of Journal Referees." *Composition Studies* 29.1 (Spring 2001): 9–26.

North, Stephen M., with Barbara A. Chepaitis, David Coogan, Lale Davidson, Ron MacLean, Cindy L. Parrish, Jonathan Post, and Beth Weatherby. *Refiguring the Ph.D. in English Studies: Writing, Doctoral Education, and the Fusion-Based Curriculum.* Urbana: NCTE, 2000.

Pemberton, Michael P. "Unstated Truths and Underpreparation in Graduate Composition Programs." Fontaine and Hunter. *Writing Ourselves into the Story.* 154–76.

Rose, Mike. *Lives on the Boundary.* NY: Penguin Books. 1989.

Scholes, Robert. *The Rise and Fall of English: Reconstructing English as a Discipline.* New Haven: Yale UP, 1998.

Preface for the Student

The Writer Who Is Not Alone: What Does Collaborative Writing Tell Us About Writing?

I wanted to reclaim [the writing for myself], but I also wanted to include what [my coauthor] wanted to do. And so I started out revising with both of those goals in mind, and what I realized, of course, is that both of the goals disappeared, and that [...] I somehow ended up with something that was not what I started with and not what he suggested, but it was just there. It was a much, much, much firmer unit and sharper than it would have been [...] and I think that's when I got a real lesson in collaborative writing.

—Pat Belanoff (Interview).

All writers know from their own experiences as writers that ideas are engendered and transformed in conversation, in collaboration, with those around us, with books we read, with stories we hear.

—Kate Ronald and Hephzibah Roskelly (264)

When you imagine yourself writing, as an advanced student or an apprentice in the field of Composition, what do you see? Where are you, and who else is there? What are you thinking about or talking about? Chances are good that many of you answer questions like these with the image of the solitary writer in your mind's eye. In an article in *College English* and in her book *Academic Writing as Social Practice* in 1987, Composition scholar Linda Brodkey described this commonly shared image as the focal point of a "scene" of writing that your reading and writing practices have taught you to envision. She writes that "The writer-writes-alone is a familiar icon of art and is perhaps most readily understood as a romantic representation of the production of canonical literature, music, painting, sculpture" ("Modernism and the Scene(s) of Writing" 396). In her book, Brodkey notes that "Whether the scene of writing is poetic or prosaic, the writer above the madding crowd in a garret, only temporarily free from family and friends in a study, or removed from the world in a library, it is the same picture—the writer writes alone" (54).

In spite of the collaborative experiences of literary artists over the past two centuries, such as those the literary scholar Jack Stillinger describes in *Multiple Authorship and the Myth of Solitary Genius,* the image of the solitary writer that was established long ago when Coleridge, Keats, Byron, and Shelley wrote has continued to be nurtured through literary history. In fact, this image is so ingrained in educational practices that more than a decade after Brodkey wrote her article, freshman writers continue to enter their college classrooms with the solitary writer as one of a set of cultural "habits of mind" that determines how they think about textual ownership and knowledge (Spigelman 234ff.).

More recently, however, composition scholars like Andrea Lunsford and Lisa Ede have begun to reflect on another image of the writer—the writer who is not alone. This writer is with one or more other writers. Sometimes these writers are together physically; other times they engage in conversation from a distance, or they continue previous conversations they've had with one another in their heads or in their personal journals. However one conjures the image of writers who are not alone, it distinguishes the solo writer from the collaborative writer: the writer who is alone in a garret, engaged in private thought, creating original ideas from the writer who is with others, consciously making ideas and creating meaning from human conversations and textual interactions.

Not surprisingly, as the image of the solo writer has dominated the minds of literary thinkers for centuries, it has also dominated research on writing and writing pedagogy. Composition as a discipline is relatively young, its beginning often demarcated by the 1966 Dartmouth conference when teachers and teachers who became researchers began to rethink where the focus of attention should be in the study of writing. As Maxine Hairston and others have noted, a dramatic shift began occurring about this time as attention was moved from the product of writing to the process. But, while Composition may have shifted its "object" of study, it didn't shift its "subject." Attention in research studies and in the writing classroom remained focused on the individual—the solo—writer. Only fairly recently have extended studies and discussions of collaborative writing begun to appear in Composition Studies. As we will discuss throughout this text, researchers like Andrea Lunsford and Lisa Ede,

Geraldine McNenny and Duane Roen, Douglas Vipond and James Reither, Anne Ruggles Gere, Karen Burke LeFevre, and others have opened the door for serious consideration of the process and value of collaborative academic writing.

However, although these authors are developing new definitions of collaborative writing and marshalling substantial arguments for its value, the grounds from which they speak have existed for quite some time. In addition to reflecting on their own experiences and the experiences of others writing collaboratively, these writers draw upon available research in psychology and philosophy to describe the practice and epistemology of collaborative writing. In this book, we intend to present you with the current culmination of this reflection and scholarship on collaborative writing. We, along with the instructor who assigned this text, believe that students who study Composition should understand collaborative writing. Other teachers, we suspect, have made arguments to you about the value of collaborative writing—that it is most like the writing you will do in the workplace, that it makes a large project more manageable, that it creates a comfortable community in an anonymous university environment. While these arguments certainly are valid, they are *not* the ones upon which we have based this text.

We believe that the larger, more encompassing argument for the value of collaborative writing is that once you truly understand collaborative writing, you will also understand something about the writing process that you didn't before. Indeed, we will go so far as to say that unless you understand collaborative writing in the way we will present it here, as an interactive process that engages participants in dialogue and the shared creation of new meanings, you cannot really understand writing. Moreover, we believe that the practice of collaborative writing can even result in better solo writing by helping writers to understand the dialogic nature of all composing such that "most good solo writing represents a single writer having some internal dialogue with herself—having more than one point of view and using more than one voice" (Elbow 12–13). In the "Preface" to her book *Revisioning Writers' Talk*, Composition scholar Mary Ann Cain illustrates the dialogic nature of solo writing when she admits that

> All writing is a social activity, but that's hard to remember when I close the office door, turn on the computer, and stare at the dark screen for hours at a time, decaf in hand. Fortunately, the conversations from which this book took shape and the relationships that enriched them were deeply sustaining—more than enough to remind me that I wasn't, after all, imprisoned in

splendid isolation but responding, initiating, talking back, listening, pausing, and, at times, letting the silence speak. (ix)

As collaborative writers ourselves—between us we have written close to ten collaborative essays or books and a myriad of conference proposals—we can provide you with an insider's perspective on this process. As other writers have done, we will draw on personal experience, excerpts from published reflections and stories and unpublished interviews with other collaborative writers, and the existing literature about dialogic collaborative writing in order to help you learn:

- how collaborative writers understand knowledge and creativity
- how and when to collaborate with another writer or writers
- how one's writing process changes from solo to collaborative writing
- how conversation becomes critically important to collaborative writers
- how collaboration can sustain writers' responses to one another and delay completion of a piece of writing
- how collaborative writers' identities and their lines of idea-ownership blur
- how creative tensions and institutional politics affect collaborative writing
- how to know whether a writer is "ready" to take on a collaborative writing project.

The discussion of these topics will be informed concurrently by theorists and practitioners. You will read about the work of theorists and historians who have studied cognitive processes of writing, human language development, and epistemological evolutions, aspects of the discipline of Composition that are most pertinent to understanding collaborative writing as a particular way of knowing and composing. You will also read excerpts from the reflections and stories of numerous academic writers who have engaged in sustained collaborative writing. Their voices, along with ours, can provide instruction and advice as you consider trying to write collaboratively.

Our goal, then, is to introduce you to the theoretical and practical aspects of collaborative writing as a dialogic, meaning-making process and to provide you with information about the discipline of Composition through the lens of collaborative writing. Along the way, we also hope to demonstrate to you the intellectual rewards we have garnered as both emerging and mature professionals when writing with others. We'll be asking you to change the situation of your composing process and to think like a collaborative writer.

As you work your way through this book, you'll discover that to write collaboratively you'll need to make an epistemic shift from the image of the writer-who-writes-alone to the image of the writer-who-writes-with-others. Instead of understanding meaning making as coming up with original ideas by yourself in some inspired moment, you'll need to be open to the possibility of creating knowledge with someone else in a shared undertaking, in a set of social interactions.

In organizing this book, we have cast the chapters as responses to questions that we as collaborative writers have asked ourselves and have heard other collaborative writing teams ask and that, we assume, would also be questions you might ask as you begin to write collaboratively.

Chapter 1: How do I need to think about knowledge and language if I am to write collaboratively?

Chapter 2: When and why should I collaborate and with whom?

Chapter 3: What changes must I make in the way I write if I am to move from solo to collaborative writing?

Chapter 4: What is the role of conversation in collaboration?

Chapter 5: How can collaborative writing help me sustain response and delay closure?

Chapter 6: How do I "co" mingle in "co" authorship?

Chapter 7: How can I manage the politics of collaborative writing?

Chapter 8: How can technology support co-writing?

Chapter 9: What more can we learn from writers who write together?

Time for Reflection

Try writing two scenes. In one, you're composing alone. What does the place look like? What are you doing, what in particular are you eating, listening to, feeling, thinking? What tools are you using to compose? In the second scene, you're composing—or talking about composing—with others. Who is there? Where are you? What is each person saying and doing? How do you feel? What do you see, notice, or need? What tools are you and the others who are with you using to do the composing? Rereading each scene, how are you a different writer in each scene? (McAndrew 98).

As we mentioned earlier, each chapter will explore one of these questions through our own and others' experiences as collaborative authors and in relation to appropriate theory and history. Each chapter will also provide you with some questions for reflection and discussion along with opportunities to try out collaborative writing for yourself.

Works Cited

Belanoff, Pat. Telephone Interview. 1 May 2000.

Brodkey, Linda. *Academic Writing as Social Practice.* Philadelphia, PA: Temple UP, 1987.

——. "Modernism and the Scene(s) of Writing." *College English* 49 (1987): 396–418.

Cain, Mary Ann. *Revisioning Writers' Talk: Gender and Culture in Acts of Composing.* Albany: State U of New York P, 1995.

Ede, Lisa, and Andrea A. Lunsford. *Singular Texts/Plural Authors: Perspectives on Collaborative Writing.* Carbondale: Southern Illinois UP, 1990.

Elbow, Peter. "Using the Collage for Collaborative Writing." *Composition Studies* 27.1 (Spring 1999): 7–14.

Gere, Anne Ruggles. *Writing Groups: History, Theory, and Implications.* Carbondale, IL: Southern Illinois UP, 1987.

Hairston, Maxine. "The Winds of Change: Thomas Kuhn and the Revolution in the Teaching of Writing." *College Composition and Communication* 33 (February 1982): 76–88.

LeFevre, Karen Burke. *Invention as a Social Act.* Carbondale: Southern Illinois UP, 1987.

McAndrew, Donald A. "That Isn't What We Did in High School: Big Changes in the Teaching of Writing." *The Subject is Writing.* Ed. Wendy Bishop. 2nd ed. Portsmouth, NH: Boynton/Cook, 1999. 91–98.

McNenny, Geraldine, and Duane H. Roen. "The Case for Collaborative Scholarship in Rhetoric." *Rhetoric Review* 10.2 (Spring 1992): 291–310.

Reither, James, and Douglas Vipond. "Writing as Collaboration." *College English* 51.8 (1989): 855–67.

Ronald, Kate, and Hephzibah Roskelly. "Learning to Take it Personally." *Personal Effects: The Social Character of Scholarly*

Writing. Ed. Deborah H. Holdstein, and David Bleich. Logan: Utah State UP, 2001. 253–66.

Spigelman, Candace. "Habits of Mind: Historical Configurations of Textual Ownership in Peer Writing Groups." *College Composition and Communication* 49.2 (May 1998): 234–55.

Stillinger, Jack. *Multiple Authorship and the Myth of Solitary Genius.* New York and Oxford: Oxford UP, 1991.

Acknowledgments

Our thanks go to the following collaborative writing partners for adding to our understanding of the motivations, roles, working methods, and attitudes that form the underpinnings of successful, dialogic collaborative writing projects in Composition Studies and for giving us their permission to include their voices in this book: Wendy Bishop of Florida State University and Hans Ostrom of the University of Puget Sound; Cy Knoblauch and Lil Brannon, both of the University of North Carolina at Wilmington; Peter Elbow of the University of Massachusetts at Amherst and Pat Belanoff of the State University of New York at Stony Brook; Kate Ronald of Miami University Ohio and Hephzibah Roskelly of the University of North Carolina at Greensboro; Peter Mortensen of the University of Illinois-Urbana and Janet Eldred of the University of Kentucky.

We also thank our editor Dickson Musslewhite and the team at Thomson Wadsworth for their support of this project and **The Wadsworth Series in Composition Studies**, their enthusiasm for our ideas and plans, and their confidence in the value of this book and the **Series** for readers new to the field of Composition Studies.

Finally, we thank Jeff Adams for his unwavering support and critical perspective and David Fontaine-Boyd for his honest interest in the collaborative work we do.

1

You Think/I Think; Therefore, We Are: How Do I Need to Think About Knowledge and Language if I Am to Write Collaboratively?

*I'm much better as a solitary writer now than I would have been
had I never collaborated. [...] You develop as an individual out
of a social relationship that you find. That's how people learn.
And collaboration is an instant proof of the way the
social construction theory works.*
—Hephzibah Roskelly (Interview)

*All of us who make meaning through writing and reading—
scholars, teachers, students—do so in community with others who
share our interests in the knowing and the knowledge-making
processes that constitute our fields of inquiry.*
—James Reither and Douglas Vipond (866)

*Knowledge emerges only through invention and re-invention,
through the restless, impatient, continuing, hopeful inquiry [people]
pursue in the world, with the world, and with each other.*
—Paulo Freire (58)

To explain language and knowledge as we believe you must in order to try out dialogic collaborative writing, in the field of Composition we routinely invoke a scenario in which you enter a parlor where a conversation is already in progress. You listen carefully so that you may join the conversation. After you leave, the conversation continues. The scene that follows has come to be known as the Burkean parlor, named after philosopher Kenneth Burke.

> Imagine that you enter a parlor. You come late. When you arrive, others have long preceded you, and they are engaged in a heated discussion, a discussion too heated for them to pause and tell you exactly what it is about. In fact, the discussion had already begun long before any of them got there, so that no one present is qualified to retrace for you all the steps that had gone before. You listen for a while, until you decide that you have caught the tenor of the argument; then you put in your oar.
>
> Someone answers; you answer him; another comes to your defense; another aligns himself against you, to either the embarrassment or gratification of your opponent, depending upon the quality of your ally's assistance. However, the discussion is interminable. The hour grows late, you must depart. And you do depart, with the discussion still vigorously in progress. (110–11)

With this parlor-metaphor, Burke intends to show how thinking is influenced by the language contexts each of you enters and how you, in turn, influence these contexts with the perspectives and experiences that you bring to them. You all enter into and out of a myriad of such social interactions—"parlors"—daily. What follows here is a recasting of the parlor scene in ways that, we think, will sound familiar and will demonstrate a rehearsal of some conversations or instances of shared meaning-making. With these two scenarios, we also intend to show you how crucial it is to understand language and knowledge as always embedded in social and collaborative practices. This understanding is crucial if you are to be open to the kinds of cognitive and social activities writing collaboratively entails—if you are to be ready to write collaboratively.

Scenario One: Listening to Others and Being Influenced by What You Hear

Imagine you are a graduate student arriving late to a party. Most of the guests are already engaged in conversation with one another, standing in small groups of four or five or in more intimate groups of two or three. Hearing familiar laughter, you see a good friend standing with three other people whom you have seen around campus but have never met before. You approach them as the laughter fades into more conversation. The only phrase that you catch, before the laughter begins again, is your friend's final words: "[...] and landed on the floor!" You stand next to your friend, smile uneasily, hoping that he will let you in on the joke or that its topic will quickly become clear through the conversation. For unless you determine what is being talked about, you can't add to the discussion or even be sure how to react appropriately to comments others are making.

Fortunately, without your conscious effort, your brain has already started to help you. Much like a computer, the brain does a kind of "search and match" process based on the bit of information it has already received. It seeks the topic of discussion by searching information that is available and appropriate given who you are (a graduate student), who you know to be engaged in the conversation you are listening to (your friend who is also a grad student), and where the conversation is taking place (a party where the guests are university students and faculty). Using "and landed on the floor" as its keywords and the situation in which they have been uttered as the context, your brain searches for potential "matches." It may come up with several possibilities: the day you dropped your tray in the student union, the time your friend tripped while giving a class lecture, and an incident in the University library last semester.

But, in the split second that your brain has begun its search, one of the group members turns to your friend and asks, "Was this during the lecture?" "Lecture" is immediately added to the keywords in your search. Some topics can now be excluded as your brain gets closer to identifying the subject of the ongoing conversation you have entered. Then, you receive the last bit of information you need. Your friend replies, "Yes, Professor Jones, this was during the discussion of literacy narratives that I was leading."

At this point, you have two key pieces of information: one that lets you verify the topic of the story as the time your friend tripped and fell during a class lecture and one that identifies a member of the conversation as a college professor. And while knowing the *topic* of the conversation is essential, the latter piece of information is equally critical. For though you are familiar with the events of the story, what details are included, excluded, emphasized, or overshadowed will depend greatly on the *context* in which the story is told. And since you originally heard this story when your friend told it to other students over lunch in the student union, you assume that telling it to a professor must have influenced its presentation. For example, you suspect that he didn't mention how he had punctuated the fall with a stifled invective or that one of the reasons he fell was because he had been so tired from the events of a long weekend. Yet both of these details had been focal points when he had told the story in the student union. Your suspicions about how the story had been presented are confirmed when Professor Jones comments that he, too, has found the lighting in that particular lecture hall to be very distracting, making shadows that can play tricks on the eyes.

Now the conversation turns to the physical hazards on campus and the difficulty of getting the University to respond to requests for repairs and improvements. Other members of the conversation add stories from their own experiences on campus. One of the women complains about the poor lighting near sidewalks and parking lots and the risks that this raises for evening students. Someone else mentions how dark the library stacks are now that the University has expanded its energy conservation program.

For the most part, you listen to the comments being made. But, at the same time, you are recalling a late afternoon class you taught last fall and how eagerly some of the young women in the class had darted out of the room when the class discussion had gone long. At the time, you had attributed their eagerness to boredom with your class. But the present conversation provides you with a new way to interpret their actions. Class had met in a building at the far end of campus; walking back through the shadowy walkways and dusky parking lots must have been disconcerting for students, particularly the women. In this context, your habit of keeping class 10 or 15 minutes overtime seems selfish rather than a mark of your intellectual rigor. And the University's interest in saving money on electricity seems extreme to the point of endangering students. You decide that this semester you will be sure to end your classes on time and to find out if any students want escorts or rides to outlying parking lots. And you might even make a phone call to the campus facilities department, urging them to increase the wattage of lights on campus.

Bringing your mind back to the conversation at hand, you find yourself nodding in agreement with your friend who concludes that using the library and computer facilities in the evening is potentially dangerous, particularly after this commuter campus becomes increasingly deserted.

When your friend had told his story in the student union, the emphasis had been on events of the weekend that resulted in his inattentive state and classroom fall. And you had joined more actively in that conversation, adding your own perspective on the events of the weekend in which you too had participated. The group of you had also shared observations about undergraduate students' commonly lethargic behavior on Monday mornings and how to adjust classroom activities either to accommodate or to take advantage of their state of mind.

Because your friend was now telling his story in a different setting and to a very different group of individuals—at a University party, in the presence of a mentor professor—the effects are also different. Because of the context of the conversation and the particular contributions and interplay of its participants, a very particular direction is taken, a particular focus emerges, and you come to think about the events of the story and your professional life in a way that you hadn't until you entered the conversation.

Time for Reflection

Recall a time when you heard a friend or relative tell a story about the same event to two very different groups. How different were the ways your friend or relative chose to tell the story? What characteristics of the audiences do you think accounted for those differences? How did the two conversations you heard play out differently?

Establishing a Position and Creating New Ideas in the Ongoing Conversation

A second scenario that follows here illustrates the deeply collaborative nature of language, the way you enter into and move between and among communities of speakers in your daily lives. Every day, each of you enters any number of parlors or ongoing spoken or written conversations. In each of these "parlors," you are involved in the two-way process of having your thinking influenced by the conversation that has preceded your entrance into the conversation and at the same time influencing the direction that the future conversation will take.

For example, in conversations that are, quite literally ongoing, like the party we have just described or a class discussion, club meeting, or family gathering, collaborative participation in the conversation is marked by routine cognitive activities: listening and responding, collecting and recollecting information, and experiencing immediate adjustments in thinking and, consequently, in comments. In the first scenario, what influenced the conversation consisted of, for the most part, recollections and experiences of the conversants. In the next scenario, we expand the influence further to include the written word as well.

Scenario Two: Making Choices When You Enter into a Conversation

Imagine being at a family reunion. Your mother complains about how crowded the local restaurants and stores become once classes begin at the nearby college. Although you could respond in several ways, you choose to mention a recent study that found undergraduate degrees to be as common and easy to acquire as high school diplomas. Given how crowded the town has become, you express your agreement with the study, adding that such overpopulation of college campuses has negative consequences that extend beyond their boundaries. Your mother glares, and suddenly you remember that your cousin, who is standing next to you, had just flunked out of college.

However, had you remembered your cousin's situation, that the summer before she started school she had had a baby and accepted a new job, you might have provided another response to the conversation, one that extended your own thinking on the subject in a different direction. You might have, for example, used the intersection of the report on college degrees and the situation your cousin was in to reflect on how many studies of college students reported in the popular media don't take into account how difficult the life of the undergraduate has become. Most have to work part- or even full-time, and many are raising families while earning their degrees. Furthermore, you add, perhaps rather than using such studies to disparage undergraduates, colleges should be designing curricula and class schedules with students' lives in mind.

Engaging at once the conversation of the moment, the texts that you have read, and your own personal perspective, your comments could extend the conversation with your mother and your own thinking about the subject at hand in several directions.

Even when each of us enters those conversations that have been ongoing for a much longer time—that have continued as individual humans develop ideas, record their thinking, respond to the thoughts and ideas that previous generations have expressed—, we can see our knowledge of a topic and our own reflections on it being powerfully influenced by the written and spoken conversations that preceded. Indeed, as we have been illustrating, knowledge—ours and that of those around us—is actually constructed in light of the conversations one enters or overhears. Through a process of assimilation and accommodation, each of us adjusts the things we hear and read to what we already believe and adjust what we believe to the things we continue to hear and read. In this way, knowledge is always under construction, always being shaped by and shaping the ideas with which it intersects.

Constructing Knowledge by Joining Ongoing Conversations

We begin our discussion of collaborative writing with these illustrations of the Burkean parlor because they provide one important basis from which to understand a conceptualization of language that is both pre-liminary and fundamental to its value. The process of meaning making that we describe here is identified by philosopher Richard Rorty and others as social construction. Composition scholar Kenneth Bruffee explains Rorty's ideas in "Collaborative Learning and the 'Conversation of Mankind,'" an essay that has become a cornerstone of the field of Composition. Bruffee writes that "Education is not a process of assimi-lating 'the truth' but, as Rorty has put it, a process of learning to 'take a hand in what is going on' by joining 'the conversation of mankind'" (647). This understanding of education and knowledge as being produc-tive and generative denies what may be more familiar to you, that is, the Cartesian formulation that knowledge is to be retrieved as a "reflection and synthesis of information about the objective world" (Bruffee 649). If you are to write collaboratively, it is essential that you understand how writing, by its very nature, enacts the social construction of knowledge. Writing collaboratively will give you a palpable experience of this process of constructing knowledge rather than retrieving it. We aim next to help you understand how to connect the social constructionist quality of knowledge with the dialogic and instrumental qualities of lan-guage. That is, the fact that language engages people in dialogue with others and that it is used as a way to understand and make meaning con-tributes to the social construction of knowledge. Speakers and writers construct knowledge out of experiences using the productive capability of language as the tool.

In the rest of this chapter, we will establish the dialogic and instru-mental quality of language and, ultimately, of thought by invoking the ideas of scholars that Composition repeatedly turns to in its continuing attempts to understand how writers produce texts as part of a social process. For it is the way in which our language and our thinking happen in necessary relation to others' words and experiences that provides the natural bedding out of which collaborative writing grows.

Writing as Dialogic

While the Burkean parlor illustrates the dialogic nature of language, there are philosophical and psychological characteristics of language that help to explain the dialogic nature of language even further. In the field of Composition, the theories about the social, dialogic qualities of spoken and written discourse that we'll call upon here to establish the epistemic and cognitive grounds of collaborative writing are also raised in other discussions about composing and pedagogy. So, in learning about these theorists in terms of collaborative writing, you'll also be learning to recognize these authorities when they are cited in other arguments to support ways of thinking and being in Composition.

To show that language by its very nature engages an individual in a conversation, a dialogue with others, we look to the Russian philosopher and literary theorist Mikhail Bakhtin. According to Bakhtin, all meanings—for our purposes, all language utterances—are part of a greater whole of meanings wherein there is constant interaction, where all meanings or utterances have the potential to influence one another (*The Dialogic Imagination* 426). And so, in as much as the "language stream" has predated all of us who use language, there are no true monologues: Every spoken or written utterance is dialogic or in dialogue with pre-occurring utterances (426). Because of this pre-existing language stream, each word we utter is partly our own and partly someone else's (345). This dialogic quality of language contributes to the process of social construction of knowledge.

But the individual is not lost in this involuntary, collaborative process. For in addition to being dialogic, actual language is also context-specific or heteroglossic. That is to say, while the dialogic nature of language results in a discourse that necessarily occurs in relation to pre-existing discourse, each utterance is specific and peculiar to the conditions in which it occurs (421). The moment the words are read/spoken/written has an influence that incorporates and supersedes the dialogue of other moments.

Another way Composition scholars have come to explain social construction is by applying the work of European psychoanalyst Julia Kristeva who herself builds on Bakhtin's idea of dialogism. Kristeva coined "intertextuality," a useful term for our purposes here that you may have come across in literature or critical theory courses. Explaining Kristeva's term, Composition scholar Richard Selzer notes that intertextuality captures the idea that discourse is always "an event, a kind of dynamic collaboration among seen and unseen writers and readers and texts, all cooperating in the creation of meaning [...] the sum of relationships materialized in discourse" (174).

When we speak or write, then, we necessarily do so in response to all that has been spoken or written before us; however, the particular moment and context in which we make our utterance assures that our discourse is unlike any that has been uttered or will be after us. So, on the one hand, our speaking and writing have essentially collaborative qualities— our meanings are conditioned and shaped by and will, in turn, condition and shape others'. But, on the other hand, ours is a dialogic language production that is unique to the moment in which it is uttered, the individual from whom it emerges, and the context within which it occurs. For instance, before writing an academic paper on feminist criticism, you may read about how feminist criticism emerged from social and cultural history, what its initial arguments posited and to whom, how it has necessarily evolved and developed its own internal controversies. If this is the portion of the feminist criticism conversation that you overhear—rather than a portion in which its roots in ancient rhetoric or its emergence as a political movement are established—you might enter the conversation by "constructing" ideas about the limitations of feminist criticism. You might integrate these ideas into your own conclusion that "the extent to which feminist criticism is tied to social and cultural history has resulted in both its intellectual value and its current acrimonious factions."

It is through entering these conversations—integrating others' topics and perspectives with your own and with others you have heard—that you make new meanings for yourselves, that you come to understand events, emotions, behaviors, and so forth, in ways that you didn't, that you couldn't have before you entered these conversations. Recall the conversation at the party: By hearing about your friend's experience in a new and very particular context, with the comments, reactions, and questions of a particular group of individuals, you came to understand something about yourself, about learning, and about students that you didn't before.

Time for Reflection

Imagine that a fellow student has asked you to explain Bakhtin's concepts and how those concepts apply to collaborative writing. Write a few sentences in which you do that. Now go back and look at what you have written in terms of dialogism itself. Identify the strands of influence in what you have written—influence from reading, writing, conversation, experiences.

Writing as Instrumental

Kenneth Bruffee, a Composition theorist and teacher whom many in Composition refer to in theorizing the work of writing centers and peer response, describes this same dialogic quality of language in his discussion of the "conversation of mankind" (sic), a conversation into which all human beings enter each time they speak or write. Bruffee claims that "knowledge is the product of humans in a state of continual negotiation or conversation" (647), a conversation that began "in primeval forests and [was] extended and made more articulate in the course of centuries. It is a conversation which goes on in public and within each of ourselves [. . .]" (Oakeshott qtd. in Bruffee 638).

Notice that where Bakhtin focuses on the dialogic qualities of *written* and *spoken* utterances, Bruffee significantly expands the argument to say that the "conversation of mankind" is equally influential on human *thought*, the conversation "within each of ourselves." For Bruffee, then, human thought is dialogic, a negotiation or conversation with pre-existing or pre-occurring exchanges. To establish this claim about the dialogic nature of human thought, Bruffee cites Russian psychologist Lev Vygotsky who demonstrates, through his study of children's language development, an interconnection between the social and instrumental qualities of speech.

According to Vygotsky, initially, *"children solve practical tasks with the help of their speech"* (26, emphasis original), using externalized speech with others to coordinate perception and action, "[they] [plan] how to solve the problem through speech and then [carry] out the prepared solution through overt action [. . .] [S]peech not only facilitates the child's effective manipulation of objects but also controls *the child's own behavior"* (26, emphasis original). As the child matures, externalized speech becomes internalized speech. Moreover, through systematic observation, Vygotsky determined that in children's developing language capacity, the greatest change is "when socialized speech (which has previously been used to address an adult) is turned inward" (27). So the child who would ask her parents how to write the letter "s" or how to put together a puzzle will turn those questions inward, reflecting on what she knows and has experienced to solve the problem by engaging in answering her own questions in her mind.

Instead of appealing to the adult, children appeal to themselves; language thus takes on an intrapersonal function in addition to its interpersonal use. When children develop a method of behavior for guiding themselves that had previously been used in relation to another person, when they organize their own activities according to a social form of behavior, they succeed in applying a social attitude to themselves. The history of the process of the internalization of social speech is also the history of the socialization of children's practical intellect (27).

In other words, initially, children direct speech to others (a form of dialogue), using language as an instrument or tool through which they can affect their own behavior—making plans and solving problems. As their language skill develops, children's externalized speech moves inward, and rather than directing their speech to someone on the outside, they direct it to themselves as they take both parts of the conversation. Yet, even though the speech has been redirected and the members of the conversation have become one, language continues to be used as an instrument to affect change. With inner speech, as with external speech, humans use language to make plans and solve problems. Collaborative writing expands this same model of knowledge-production and problem-solving by taking the process one step further to *re*-externalize inner speech. The previously internalized questions about what to write, how to write it, where to begin, and so forth become questions that the collaborative writers ask one another and solve together.

Not All Writing Is Collaborative, but Collaboration Is at the Heart of All Writing

And so we arrive at the structural and rhetorical equivalence between thought and language and, consequently, their equivalently collaborative qualities. The work of Bakhtin, Bruffee, and Vygotsky help to explain how all instances of language and thought occur in relation to other instances of language and thought. Return to the Burkean parlor; recall the instances in which spoken and written language was affected by pre-existing language. The words you think, write, and speak are partly your own and partly someone else's—the meanings that you utter or think are influenced in deep, even unidentifiable ways in the course of their coming to be by the stream of conversations in which you, as language users, exist.

We seem to have reached the point of defining all writing as collaborative, to be offering no distinction between the process of writing alone and writing together. But those of us who have written with others know quite well that there are tremendous differences between these two processes, specifically in how, when, where, and why these processes happen and how others receive and judge their products. Our goal in this chapter has not been to establish that all writing is collaborative writing; rather, we want to define for you the theory about the nature and development of language from which selected instances of collaborative writing organically grow. That is, collaborative writing is compatible with the profile of language that we have been drawing—as a conversation, a dialogue, a tool for solving problems. Indeed, the more common image of the writing process—that of a writer who writes alone—belies the social, instrumental, collaborative nature of language.

To understand collaborative writing as we are proposing, you must also understand the nature of written language and knowledge making as we have described them. That is, we ask you to imagine the writer who writes with others as engaged in the recursive, two-way, turn-taking process of sustained, ongoing conversation and dialogue. To think otherwise makes collaborative writing an aberrant activity tacked on to a curriculum or turned to when writers are lonely or blocked rather than a writing process that grows out of the very nature of language.

Trying Out Collaborative Writing

Working with a group of at least three other students, on a sheet of paper and so the others can't see, write a sentence that you imagine could begin a brief fictional scene. Then hand the paper to the person next to you who will read your sentence silently, writes a follow-up sentence, folds your sentence over so that it cannot be seen, and passes the paper on to the next person in the group. This person reads the second sentence only, writes a sentence to follow up to the second, folds the second over, and passes on the paper with only his sentence showing. Keep doing this, letting the next writer see only the previously written sentence, until you have generated about 15–20 sentences. Once this is done, open the whole sheet and read all of the sentences.

Briefly write what you observe about the nature of this collaborative writing and the "text" that this process generated.

Works Cited

Bakhtin, Mikhail M. *The Dialogic Imagination*. Trans. Caryl Emerson and Michael Holquist. Austin: U of Texas P, 1981.

Bruffee, Kenneth. "Collaborative Learning and 'The Conversation of Mankind.'" *College English* 46.7 (November 1984): 635–52.

Burke, Kenneth. *The Philosophy of Literary Form: Studies in Symbolic Action.* Baton Rouge: Louisiana State UP, 1967.

Freire, Paulo. *The Pedagogy of the Oppressed.* New York: Continuum, 1986.

McNenny, Geraldine, and Duane H. Roen. "The Case for Collaborative Scholarship in Rhetoric and Composition." *Rhetoric Review* 10.2 (Spring 1992): 291–310.

Reither, James A., and Douglas Vipond. "Writing as Collaboration." *College English* 51.8 (1989): 855–67.

Roskelly, Hephzibah. Personal Interview. 14 April 2000.

Selzer, Jack. "Intertextuality and the Writing Process: An Overview." *Writing in the Workplace: New Research Perspectives.* Ed. Rachel Spilka. Carbondale: Southern Illinois UP, 1993. 171–80.

Vygotsky, Lev S. *Thought and Language.* Cambridge: MIT, 1962.

For Further Reading

Bakhtin, Mikhail. *Speech Genres and Other Late Essays.* Trans. Caryl Emerson and Michael Holquist. Austin: U of Texas P, 1986.

Barthes, Roland. "From Work to Text." *Textual Strategies: Perspectives in Post-Structuralist Criticism.* Ed. J. V. Harari. Ithaca: Cornell UP, 1979. 73–81.

Bruner, Jerome. *Actual Minds, Possible Worlds.* Cambridge: Harvard UP, 1986.

Farmer, Frank. *Saying and Silence: Listening to Composition with Bakhtin.* Logan: Utah State UP, 2001.

Foucault, Michel. "What is an Author?" *Textual Strategies: Perspectives in Post-Structuralist Criticism.* Ed. J. V. Harari. Ithaca: Cornell UP, 1979. 141–60.

Inge, M. Thomas. "Collaboration and Concepts of Authorship." *PMLA* 116.3 (2001): 623–30.

Kristeva, Julia. *Desire in Language.* Ed. L. S. Roudiez. Trans. T. Gora, A. Jardine, and L. Roudiez. New York: Columbia UP, 1980.

Leonard, James S., et al., eds. *Author-ity and Textuality: Current Views of Collaborative Writing.* West Cornwall, CT: Locust Hill P, 1994.

McComiskey, Bruce. *Teaching Composition as a Social Process.* Logan, UT: Utah State UP, 2000.

Romano, Tom. "Writing Through Others: The Necessity of Collaboration." *Vital Signs 2: Teaching and Learning Language Collaboratively.* Ed. James L. Collins. Portsmouth, NH: Heinemann Boynton/Cook, 1991. 3–12.

Stillinger, Jack. *Multiple Authorship and the Myth of Solitary Genius.* New York: Oxford UP, 1991.

Thralls, Charlotte. "Bakhtin, Collaborative Partners, and Published Discourse: A Collaborative View of Composing." *New Visions of Collaborative Writing.* Ed. Janis Forman. Portsmouth, NH: Heinemann Boynton/Cook, 1992. 63–81.

Trimbur, John. "Consensus and Difference in Collaborative Learning." *College English* 51 (October 1989): 602–16.

2

Choosing-Up Partners: When and Why Should I Collaborate and with Whom?

But I think we learned just about how we clicked very early. [...]
We managed to bring ourselves about as far apart as we could,
to Nebraska and Boston. And so the first time we wrote together
for publication, the first time we presented together, was really
an attempt to keep working together. [...] all of those things [team
teaching, being co-administrators] were in some ways kind of
writing together, and so when we started writing together, it
really wasn't a big wrench for us to figure out how to do it.
Because we knew each other, trusted each other, had heard
each other's words [...] and read each other's writing.
—Kate Ronald and Hephzibah Roskelly (Interview)

So we were writing together because we happened to be together,
but I think the decision to do the textbook depended upon [...]
our feeling that we could trust each other and that we [...] could
let each other revise. [...] So in a sense, we set out to create some-
thing in a genre that [...] we had negative feelings about [...].
The decision to write together came from wanting to produce
one of these things, and well, clearly, I couldn't do it alone.
And we wanted to have a textbook [A Community of Writers]
that embodied our take on writing.
—Peter Elbow and Pat Belanoff (Interview)

When, Why, and With Whom?—Which Comes First?

We begin this chapter by assuming that—if you're still reading with interest and curiosity—you've decided that the process of constructing knowledge socially makes sense to you—either because you've actually participated in this process or because you want to try setting this process in motion to test it out. In reality, as collaborative writing pairs Kate Ronald and Hephzibah Roskelly and Peter Elbow and Pat Belanoff recount in the epigraphs here, writers don't first decide that they'll collaborate and next find someone to collaborate with about something, even though we've been writing as if that's the sequence of choices. We don't much like the fact that that's the way instruction in collaboration often occurs in writing courses: For example, a writing teacher might claim that because collaborative writing is prevalent in the workplace, students need to team up to work on a writing assignment together. We didn't do much better at representing the way collaborative writing happens when we originally drafted this chapter with the following instructions:

> Once you've decided to try out collaborative writing as a process of making meaning, you'll need a writing partner who shares your interests and motivation to compose something collaboratively and shares your view of collaborative writing. You'll also need "something" to write about and a rhetorical situation for which to write it.

Both sets of instructions—the typical writing instructor's and ours— belie the way collaborative writing happens. And so, the three questions of this chapter—"When and why should I collaborate and with whom?"—present us with a chicken-and-the-egg problem of sorts: Which of the three comes first? As you'll see from our own experiences and those of other collaborative writing pairs, a whole lot of conversation and getting to know one another professionally and personally precedes the actual decision to write collaboratively. The four scenarios that follow here will help you understand why, when, and with whom collaborative writing takes place. There's no one way that collaborative writing happens—no magic formula. But there are some common threads that tie these accounts together. In future chapters, we'll continue to draw from retrospective narratives by academics who choose to write together to mine them for other distinguishing characteristics— challenges, processes, and rewards—of collaborative writing. Now we ask that you try to discover the multiple ways to answer the three questions of the chapter that are embedded in these narratives.

Scenario One: Our Story

Here's how we remember the start of our own collaborative history: More than fifteen years ago, we led parallel lives as Writing Center Director and Freshman Writing Director at two private colleges in a consortium on idyllic campuses across the street from each other, beneath the San Gabriel mountains in southern California. We first met at a gathering of writing instructors from the five Claremont Colleges. That meeting led to many long lunches and afternoon coffee breaks during which we talked about the politics of our situations at institutions where teaching writing and doing research in Composition were marginalized. We first decided to write together in response to a call for proposals for the Conference on College Composition and Communication (CCCC) that we both wanted our institutions to pay for us to attend. The call for proposals led us to formulate a panel based on our shared perceptions about the ways that our teaching and administrative lives at these private colleges were left out of the political agenda of Composition Studies in the late 1980s. Once we'd conceptualized the panel (that is, in Susan's terms, once we'd come up with a title for it that really captured what the panel was about, "Unprivileged Voices in the Academy of the Privileged"), we invited, John, a writing program administrator from the women's college in the consortium, to join us. His acceptance assured us that our concept was plausible, and his contribution expanded its reach. The panel was accepted for the 1989 program in Seattle.

The pattern of inviting others to join us continued as we co-wrote a grant proposal for a Writing Institute with John and now Jackie, representing a fourth college in the consortium. We kept asking each other: "Were we the only ones feeling this way?" Funding for the Institute supported writing-across-the-disciplines workshops, a newsletter, and a regional conference "Composing Ourselves and Our Discipline," named after Andrea Lunsford's chair's address at the 1989 CCCC. By extending our collaborative writing effort to include others, we affirmed that indeed we were not "the only ones feeling this way." And so we came up with the idea for an edited collection, again clearly conceptualized once we agreed on the title: *Writing Ourselves into the Story: Unheard Voices from Composition Studies*. Our call for proposals increased our community and allowed us to extend our collaborative writing efforts to include other writers.

We culled chapters for the book while watching the Persian Gulf War unfold on CNN. (Ironically, now we are revising this chapter as the war in Iraq unfolds on CNN.) With this edited collection, we took on another purpose that we would remain engaged by: to define our profession or discipline more inclusively and expansively. Airplane and lunchtime conversations led to conference proposals for CCCC panels and two journal articles: one on rendering the conversation of Composition and another that initiated a symposium on peer review. A second co-edited collection on ethics came out of panel presentations at NCTE and the CCCC.

Time for Reflection

Write a profile of someone with whom because of exigency or proximity you might actually decide to write collaboratively.

Explicating Our Collaborative History

Since that first time and that first professional context, both our academic lives have become separate, fast-paced, hectic, and demanding—secure and tenured—different from what we ever imagined during those idyllic days in Claremont, California, when we led parallel lives. We're both teaching in English departments at different universities now, large state universities in California and Georgia. We are no longer able to connect across lunch in a café or paper-strewn floors and conference tables; we no longer sit at a keyboard and in front of a computer screen together.

Still, the die had been cast; we were hooked: We remain intellectually and emotionally connected by the habit of writing together that we began cultivating more than a decade ago. Now, separated by time zones and geographical distance, although the ways we accomplish it have changed physically and evolved technologically, we value writing collaboratively too much ever to consider abandoning it. "Why?" Because from doing it, we have learned so much about what it means to write and think together, and we still want to get even better at writing together.

For us, the answer to "With whom?" remains firmly anchored in this shared commitment that began with those conversations way back when we were trying to carve out places for ourselves in the profession. We realized several projects into our collaborative history that in our first decision to write collaboratively with each other for the CCCC panel proposal lay the elements of all our future decisions to write with each other and to invite others to write with us: an intellectual and emotional connection that derived from a shared perception about our professional lives that was not being given voice to in the scholarship of our field and a desire to seek out other voices who would identify with our perception. And so, even in this book you'll find rendered and invoked the voices and stories of others like us whom we sought out for interviews, conversations, and e-mail exchanges when we decided to explicate the value of writing together for newcomers to the field of Composition Studies.

In retrospect, we realize that the answer to "When?" is driven by our continual building upon one genre and rhetorical context to get to another. We engage in a shuttling re-conceptualization process as we move from genre to genre. That first panel presentation—after collaborative revision, a rejection, and further collaborative revision—was eventually published as a journal article. The theme and the conversations at the regional conference we coordinated led to the prospectus for our first edited collection, the call for proposals, and its eventual publication as a book. This pattern of conceptualizing and re-conceptualizing projects for various rhetorical contexts has become a mainstay of our professional lives because it allows us not to settle for an ending to a line of questioning that we find compelling. By writing together, we continually revise our ideas, pushing them farther conceptually and increasing their range and impact in more than one professional rhetorical context.

Scenario Two: Singular Texts/Plural Authors

The story of Andrea Lunsford and Lisa Ede's professional writing collaboration has become canonical in the field of Composition Studies. In fact, their groundbreaking research on collaboration and authorship in *Singular Texts/Plural Authors: Perspectives on Collaborative Writing* published in 1990, forms the background or source from which all other stories of dialogic collaborative writing flow. Colleagues at Ohio State University, Ede and Lunsford began writing in the early 1980s because of shared intellectual interests and the fact that they are friends who enjoy being together, even if most of that time is spent working on writing projects together: "The simple physical act of meeting to work [...] has come to serve as a powerful writing ritual for both of us" (126). When each had moved on to a different university position, their "need to be physically together at certain crucial times in [their] composing process require[d] careful planning" (126). Lunsford and Ede describe the "how" of their coauthoring as "talking, trading texts (one of our favorite collaborative strategies is to revise one another's writing), asking questions." If they're stuck, they'll "work together on the same text, passing a single pad of paper back and forth, one of us completing the sentence or paragraph that the other began. By the time that most essays are finished, we simply couldn't say that 'Lisa wrote this section, while Andrea wrote that' " (126).

Scenario Three: Collaborwriting

When another pair of college teachers Hal Blythe and Charlie Sweet talk about their "collaborwriting"—a term we wish we had coined—they describe the process of writing together regularly, five days a week, forty-eight weeks a year in a booth at a Kentucky McDonald's. Writing this way for over twenty years, they have been published in a variety of genres ranging from crime mysteries to academic articles. They get their ideas for a murder mystery or a critical essay on poetry from a habit of informal brainstorming conversation that draws on experiences and information they've each been absorbing. They're always in the midst of more than one writing project: "Besides the primary piece we're bringing to a boil on any given day, we like to have a second starting to bubble, and a third we've just put on the stove" (40). Leading intersecting rather than parallel lives in the same department at Eastern Kentucky University, they are able to plan their schedules to accommodate their collaborwriting habits. Enviably, they are able to "write every word facing each other across the paper-filled Formica" (41) of the McDonald's booth—a truly dialogic, generative process.

Why have Blythe and Sweet been so motivated to write together for so long? Certainly, they collaborwrite because they're like-minded colleagues and friends. But their motivation extends beyond the ease of collegiality and friendship. They have found that in writing together they can avoid a lot of the pitfalls of solo composing. They socialize rather than feeling isolated, converse with each other rather than thinking and writing alone with no one to talk to except oneself. They get constant support and criticism from one another. They never procrastinate or suffer from writer's block, false starts, or burnout.

Time for Reflection

Interview a student or professor whose work you respect about his or her experience with collaborative writing—why they decided to write with someone else or why they decided not to.

Scenario Four: Women's Ways

A fourth touchstone for the kind of collaborative writing we describe in this book is Mary Field Belenky's story of dialogic collaboration among four developmental psychologists that produced the groundbreaking *Women's Ways of Knowing: The Development of Self, Voice, and Mind*—academic writing that's figured prominently in research in writing pedagogy since its publication in 1986. In all the other accounts in this chapter, we see that friendship and proximity can be a mode of operation that may lead to collaborative writing. Belenky notes that, initially, it wasn't friendship or proximity that drew the four psychologists together. Instead, it was a common research interest that brought them together. All four shared a commitment to investigate the ways that women develop intellectually and ethically. They discovered that they were like-minded colleagues in the process of brainstorming a research design and grant proposal together. Their conversations at a pajama-party meeting at a New Hampshire motel led the four to write a proposal that was funded by FIPSE. The grant supported pajama-party meetings every five weeks for three years. Belenky describes a working situation similar to Blythe and Sweet's—the "luxury" of "sustained conversation":

> Very regularly, then, every five or six weeks, we were able to sit down together and work around the clock for three or four days at a time. I can't tell you how important it is to have this kind of time for working, sleeping on your thought, and returning to the conversation—without distractions from children and telephones. (30)

The plan and format of the book took shape during "a month-long pajama party at a cottage on the shore, a big rambling mansion on the ocean" (31). While they divided up the chapters to be drafted individually, the four coauthors decided to strive for merging their four voices into one by not putting their names on individual pieces. This attitude toward authorship reflects the way the four tapped the power of conversation and writing together to construct knowledge.

Time for Reflection

In your journal or notebook, take one of the four scenarios as a model and insert yourself and your writing partner into it. After you've done this, can you identify anything in this chapter that would prevent you or dissuade you from trying collaborative writing. Why?

Summary: When, Why, and with Whom?

These four scenarios—some version of which may sound familiar or attractive to you—offer some key ingredients, or a framework, for deciding when, why, and with whom to write collaboratively. More often than not, you might conclude that collaborative writing happens by serendipity for, to a large extent, our stories of how writers choose-up partners derive from their being in the right places at the right times and open to opportunities for connecting with like-minded colleagues. You might also conclude that a personal relationship and a feeling of trust are essential to any successful collaborative writing team. That's not to say that writing pairs are always "best friends." But they must have the potential for a professional chemistry that is supported or encouraged by a personal connection. If you don't enjoy talking to one of your colleagues over lunch about professional issues, it's safe to say that you probably won't want to write with him or her either.

You may decide to write collaboratively when you find someone who shares your annoyances or who is surprised or pleased by similar professional experiences. The reason for being bothered by the same rules or concepts or theories or practices may not be the same for both writers, but they begin with the same reason to write—to figure out how to understand and get rid of the annoyance. You are pleased to find out that you aren't alone in your feelings, and the collaboration grows, in part, from this discovered camaraderie and from a new goal: to find others like the two of you or to convince others to join the two of you in your shared perspective. You may decide to write collaboratively when someone challenges you to join them in writing about something that you alone or both of you together have complained about forever, when the discussions reach a point that going public seems right, seems the next step. You may decide to write collaboratively when you find yourselves nearby individuals who have the same professional needs as you have—to be professionally active. Sometimes, asking someone across the street or down the hall in your department is an easier option than writing alone or finding someone outside your campus. Proximity can encourage collaborative writing. You may decide to write collaboratively when professional genres either encourage or require a form of collaboration. Ede and Lunsford call these "assignments" or "invitations." We too may respond to a call for proposals, but it's our own impetus to work on some project that we feel strongly about that makes us respond. A conference or workshop proposal form includes spaces for multiple presenters. In the lore of our profession, we know that it is easier to get panels and workshops accepted than individual presentations. Actually, it may just be expedient that multi-voiced proposals are valued more than individual ones because it saves the conference organizers time. So we write collaboratively in order to fit the requirements or the implications about what is valued and what counts more. You may decide to write collaboratively when you find someone with whom you share some basic, important conceptual frameworks or sensibilities but with whom you also differ enough—in professional position, gender, past experience—that, as a pair you don't simply mirror one another. This element of difference in the decision to write collaboratively guarantees that the whole will be greater than the sum of its parts. In order to allow the thinking and writing to reach a third point—in order to be open to making meaning,—collaborative writers can, to borrow psychologist Jerome Bruner's term, "scaffold" one another. Coauthors can challenge each other about ideas and rhetoric, supporting each other to reach toward making meaning previously unknown. Collaboration is what Vygotsky might call one of the tools that we use to think and learn, not just when we're novice writers but also when we're experienced solo authors who have decided to write collaboratively.

Andrea Lunsford and Lisa Ede have captured Vygotsky's idea and described what may be the primary motive for all of us who write together to continue to do so despite any number of challenges. The ultimate answer to "Why?" for us, for Blythe and Sweet, for Belenky, Clinchy, Goldberger, and Tarule, for Lunsford and Ede is that "[...] our joint ideas and understandings enable us, via the crucible of our conversations and collaboration, to discover new meanings—meanings simply not available to us working alone" (126). With its connotations of "testing" and "melting together," "crucible" is yet another metaphor like the Burkean parlor for the social construction of knowledge. Conversation and collaboration act as tests of belief and as ways of melting together the materials of two (or more) minds into something previously unknown.

Trying Out Collaborative Writing

Design a collaborative writing project with an ideal coauthor that you've fabricated or with a real one that you've decided to write with.

Works Cited

Ashton-Jones, Evelyn, and Dene Kay Thomas. "Composition, Collaboration, and Women's Ways of Knowing: A Conversation with Mary Belenky." *(Interviews): Cross-Disciplinary Perspectives on Rhetoric and Literacy.* Ed. Gary A. Olson and Irene Gale. Carbondale: Southern Illinois UP, 1991. 27–44.

Blythe, Hal, and Charlie Sweet. "Collaborwriting." Waldrep 39–43.

Bruner, Jerome. "The Role of Dialogue in Language Acquisition." *The Child's Conception of Language.* Ed. A. Sinclair, R. J. Jsarvella, and J. M. Levelt. New York: Springer-Verlag, 1978. 241–56.

Ede, Lisa, and Andrea A. Lunsford. *Singular Texts/Plural Authors: Perspectives on Collaborative Writing.* Carbondale: Southern Illinois UP, 1990.

Elbow, Peter, and Pat Belanoff. Telephone Interview. 1 May 2000.

Fontaine, Sheryl I., and Susan Hunter. *Writing Ourselves Into the Story: Unheard Voices from Composition Studies.* Carbondale: Southern Illinois UP, 1993.

Fontaine, Sheryl I., Susan Hunter, and John Peavoy. "Unprivileged Voices in the Academy of the Privileged." *Freshman English News* 19 (Fall 1990): 2–9.

Lunsford, Andrea, and Lisa Ede. "Collaboration and Compromise: The Fine Art of Writing with a Friend." Volume II. Waldrep 121–27.

Ronald, Kate, and Hephzibah Roskelly. Personal Interview. 14 April 2000.

Vygotsky, Lev S. *Thought and Language.* Cambridge: MIT, 1962.

Waldrep, Tom, ed. *Writers on Writing.* New York: Random House, 1985.

——. *Writers on Writing.* Volume II. New York: Random House, 1988.

For Further Reading

Day, Kami, and Michele Eodice. *(First Person)²: A Study of Coauthoring in the Academy.* Logan: Utah State UP, 2001.

Fontaine, Sheryl I. "With Writers' Eyes: Perception and Change in Manuscript Review Procedures." *Rhetoric Review* 13.2 (Spring 1995): 259–64.

Fontaine, Sheryl I., and Susan M. Hunter, eds. *Foregrounding Ethical Awareness in Composition and English Studies.* Portsmouth, NH: Heinemann Boynton/Cook, 1998.

———. "Rendering the 'Text' of Composition." *Journal of Advanced Composition* 12.2 (Fall 1992): 395–406.

Hunter, Susan M. "The Case for Reviewing as Collaboration and Response." *Rhetoric Review* 13.2 (Spring 1995): 265–69.

Hutcheon, Linda, and Michael Hutcheon. "A Convenience of Marriage: Collaboration and Interdisciplinarity." *PMLA* 116.5 (October 2001): 1364–76.

Leonardi, Susan J., and Rebecca A. Pope. "(Co)Labored Li(v)es; or, Love's Labors Queered." *PMLA* 116.3 (May 2001): 631–37.

Ronald, Kate, and Hephzibah Roskelly. "Learning to Take It Personally." *Personal Effects: The Social Character of Scholarly Writing*. Ed. Deborah H. Holdstein, and David Bleich. Logan: Utah State UP, 2001. 253–66.

CHAPTER

3

1 + 1 > 2: What Changes Must I Make When I Move from Solo to Collaborative Writing?

I would rather collaborate than write alone; though I find myself writing alone a lot. Writing alone is easier in many ways. It takes less time for one thing.

—Lil Brannon (E-mail)

In terms of process, I doubt if we've changed each other all that much—I'm talking about the basic day-to-day habits of a writer. What's interesting to me is that the personal habits have little if any negative effect on our collaborations. The influence for me comes when I write poems or criticism or scholarly things alone—I know darn well I've picked up perspectives via osmosis from [Wendy]—ideas, habits of experimentation, rhetorical moves.

—Hans Ostrom (E-mail)

Dividing the Tasks and Assembling the Products

Imagine your most familiar "collaborative writing" experience. Most likely, it was a classroom experience that appeared on a syllabus as "group project" somewhere midway or more through the semester. The class instructor made the group assignments either from randomly drawn lots, a list created on the basis of some mysterious sorting system (writers of the same or mixed caliber, equally driven or mixed-achieving level students, students with similarly declared interests, and so forth), or the risky but popular student self-selection method. The instructor either determined and assigned a general subject area within which each group was to define a topic or, limiting choice further, the instructor assigned each group a particular topic of study. The final product was a written document with particularly defined sections or an oral presentation with "parts" for each member. And it is likely that your individual grade was closely tied to your participation in the group or replaced with a single grade for each group.

The first time your group met, things were a bit uncomfortable, especially if you didn't know one another. Maybe there was some grousing: "Not another group project!" or "What does the instructor expect us to do?" Finally, after the group meandered around for awhile, rereading the assignment and making jokes, one group member took charge: "OK, so how are we going to get this done?" At this point, there may have been discussion about what had to happen in order for the assignment to be completed—what had to be written, how many people needed to be responsible for each section, what order the work should happen in, and what deadlines had to be set. The self-assigned "leader" collected phone numbers and e-mail addresses and solicited group members' available work times. The other members of the group fell into roles according to personality and experience: a first lieutenant to assist the leader, a group entertainer who continued to joke around and wander off-task, a note-taker who volunteered or was volunteered by someone else who wanted to avoid the task, a loner self-identified by his or her silence and sullen agreement. With roles in place, the leader orchestrated the designation and selection of actual writing tasks, how the work would be divided and distributed. Once the tasks had been identified and parceled out, the group members went their separate ways, and, from then on, any "collaboration" took place during periodic meetings at which members reported on their individual progress and a final meeting or two at which the various pieces of writing were assembled. In the end, the group was deemed successful if all members completed their individual assignments with equal effort and quality and if a single, completed product was assembled from the individual pieces of writing.

Lunsford and Ede would categorize such a collaborative experience as "hierarchical"; that is, it is organized in a linear fashion, structured by the roles of each participant, and driven by the goal of accomplishing a particularly defined task (235). After assigning roles, members of the group work independently of one another, coming together occasionally for progress reports and, finally, to assemble the pieces of product supplied by each member. In fact, because situations like these rely so much on independent work, they can be labeled as "cooperative" rather than "collaborative" (Yancey and Spooner 50). That is, their success depends on the degree to which group members can cooperatively coordinate individual writing assignments with one another to achieve a shared goal of completing a task.

Cooperative writing appears to require little change or adaptation on the part of individual writers who, once writing tasks have been defined among group members, actually write their parts alone, solo. The most apparent changes are procedural ones that occur when the overall writing task must be divided up among multiple writers. Rather than one solo writer completing the whole project, then, multiple solo writers spin off with each completing a portion of the whole before returning to attach it to or fit it in with the others' portions.

But, if this division of labor is the only change necessary for cooperative writing experiences to be successful, then what accounts for the high occurrence of group projects that don't succeed? Ask yourself how many successful group projects you have participated in. Their lack of success is commonly due to the fact that the very structure of a cooperative experience can serve to encourage members' belief in the existence of the solo, independent, asocial writer—a belief that often works to erode group members' commitment to and production of a common, shared project. When cooperative writing experiences are successful, it is most likely because in spite of their belief in the solo creative experience, the writers coincidentally share an overriding intellectual investment in the quality and quantity of their work. Or, the writers—consciously or not—embrace an image of the writer that is contrary to that of the writer alone, silent, cut off from the world, and chained to the blank screen or page.

Time for Reflection

Recall a time when you were assigned a collaborative writing project. Write about how the assignment was structured, what was expected of each group member, and how successfully the goal of the group was accomplished. Write, too, about why these parts were or were not successful.

Changing Your Mental Image of the Writer

The image of the lonely, garretted writer is easy for most individuals in English Studies to conjure. It may even be the image that attracted them to the study of literature: the lone, perhaps lonely and usually male writer, working selflessly to translate the words of his Muse into a masterpiece. Bruffee believes that graduate training in English has taught students that any other image would be not only foreign to the discipline, but inappropriate ("Collaborative Learning and the 'Conversation of Mankind'" 645). Consider, now, the significance that such an image holds for one's understanding of collaborative writing. That is, if writing is believed to be the activity of individual, independent minds, then the possibility of two or more people writing together is difficult to imagine. Bruffee describes the way most members of the profession think about collaborative writing:

> Most of us are not in the habit of thinking about writing nonfoundationally as a collaborative process, a distanced or displaced conversation among peers in which we construct knowledge. We tend to think of writing foundationally as a private, solitary, "expressive" act in which language is a conduit from a solitary mind to a solitary mind. (*Collaborative Learning* 54)

It is not only teachers of literature who are responsible for planting this image of writing in students' minds. As Linda Brodkey explains, in spite of available research to the contrary, teachers of writing promote the same image in the minds' eye of novice writers:

> Those who teach as well as those who take composition courses are influenced by the scene of writing, namely, that all of us try to recreate a garret and all that it portends whether we are writing in a study, a library, a classroom, or at a kitchen table, simply because we learned this lesson in writing first. Further, those of us who have since learned no other lessons, who can image no pictures of writing other than the writer-writes-alone, are the most likely to pass that lesson on to a new generation and are the least likely to reconceptualize writing in any of the ways it is being represented by research in composition. (397)

Holding onto and nurturing the image of the writer-writes-alone cannot only impede the success of writers working together but can completely undermine the value of collaboration. In fact, getting rid of this image is the single most significant change that writers must make as they move from solo to collaborative writers. Those who engage in the kind of cooperative writing that we described at the opening of this chapter may be able to circumvent failure and find ways to get the work done in spite of this image. However, for those who engage in *true* collaborative writing—a "dialogic" collaboration where members' roles are loosely defined and structured, shifting as the collaboration unfolds— success can happen only if the image of the solo writer is replaced with the image of a social, interactive, writer-in-the-world. Moreover, when writers exchange the image of the writer-writes-alone for that of a writer-in-the world, they naturally find that the creative and generative value in the ensuing collaborative give and take, listen and respond, say and say-back processes of articulating and defining goals supersedes the value of the goals themselves (Lunsford and Ede 235).

While it may seem hard to believe that the mental image or picture writers hold can have such an impact on their actions, Brodkey explains that a mental image is much more than a static picture we carry in our mind's eye: "It is not enough to say this is a picture, for such pictures provide us with a vocabulary for thinking about and explaining writing to ourselves and one another" (349). Citing Kenneth Burke, Brodkey claims that any "representative anecdote" that constitutes our mental picture, "generates ideology" (401). And so, it may not be merely writing procedures that must be changed in the shift from solo to collaborative writer, but the very ideology or theory of writing one embraces. Writers who hold fast to the ideology that writing is an asocial, solitary process will limit themselves to a form of writing that is, at best, cooperative, not collaborative.

If we are correct, you are being acculturated to a profession in which, despite research that would support a contrary representation, the image of the writer-writes-alone has been passed on from generation to generation of student. In fact, as Candace Spigelman's research with peer writing groups shows, students continue to enter writing classrooms with notions of "autonomous originality and private production" firmly entrenched (71). And such an image is more than just a picture you carry in your mind's eye, "it provides us with a vocabulary for thinking about and explaining writing to ourselves and to one another" (Brodkey 349). Because you can engage in hierarchical collaboration and still hold onto your belief that writing is a solo, individual, independent activity—work with your group but then return to your garret where you create your own ideas and embed them within your own sentences—the need for a change in ideology can be easily overlooked. And even once you agree to such a need, you cannot change ingrained images and well-accepted ideologies by blinking your eyes and willing it so. The change will occur only if you look closely at the kind of research outlined in Chapter 6 that supports this ideological change and consider the consequences such a change would have to the teaching of writing as well as the way you write. Finally, if you are to engage in true, dialogic collaboration, you must exchange this scene of writing for another. For dialogic collaboration emerges from a genuine belief that all writing is, by its very nature, a collaborative activity, that it is social and naturally includes other people and other writers.

Consider the following notes written by three students about their collaborative writing experience. Notice how these students—Deb, Tracey, and Kathy—get beyond dividing up tasks and use the computer to help them move from solo to collaborative writing. Notice how Kathy's retrospective account dramatizes that what began as cooperative writing became an instance of dialogic collaborative writing:

> We began with a dialogue on the computer. We took turns writing observations and responses about our books over the courses of a week or so during our free periods and after school. We didn't talk to each other in person about what we were writing; we just wrote and responded on the computer. [...] I felt Deb and Tracey were a "safe" audience and I knew much of what I was writing was going to be scrapped, so I felt free to just ramble on about whatever happened to come to mind.
>
> The next step was to print out a hard copy which we then went over in class. [...] We made a list of what seemed to be the most important points we wanted to cover in the actual book review. We came up with a total of six points which we divided between the three of us. Once we had our assignments we worked individually on them, then brought our work together and merged it onto one disk.
>
> Maybe the most important part of our collaboration was the conclusion, since it is the only part of the paper that we truly wrote together. Tracey and I had each written a paragraph that would have served as a conclusion. Deb and Tracey experimented with brand new conclusions for 15 to 20 minutes while I typed. They were both getting frustrated, so I joined them when I finished. I suggested we make a list of what points we wanted to make in the conclusion, so we brainstormed for five minutes. Then we all started throwing out lines and writing down the ones we liked. After we had a few of them, I moved over to the computer and asked to read back what we had come up with so far. I typed it in and they looked over my shoulder. We read it out loud and spent about twenty minutes changing a word here, a phrase there, trying to tie our points together. (Reckendorf qtd. in Elbow and Belanoff 95–97)

Time for Reflection

Draw a diagram or tell the story of something you recently wrote. Start at what you consider to have been the very beginning, include as many moments in the process as you can recall. Once you are done, go back and indicate all of the moments that involved other people. Next, working in small groups of 1–4 members, explain to one another the diagram of your writing process that you created for the last writing activity assignment. Then, using your experiences as your source of information, make some generalizations about the way other people are integrated into solo writing activities.

Moving Apart and Coming Together

We have explained the changes in ideology that occur in the shift to being a collaborative writer and the ways in which conversation, in the context of this new ideology, comes to play a defining role in the process. Now, consider the value of working with other individuals who have skills, experience, and knowledge that is different from your own and the implications of this value for your writing. Although solo writers may have conversations with others throughout their composing process, they don't engage in the same degree of interaction as collaborative writers. For the latter, the interaction becomes a process in and of itself, one that Jerome Bruner, building on Lev Vygotsky's notion of a "zone of proximal development," identified as "scaffolding."

As workers build or repair a large building, together they create a parallel structure called a scaffold. From this scaffold, itself a fairly intricate and highly durable piece of workmanship, the construction crew reaches out to build, resurface, paint, and repair the main structure. Unlike a ladder, which comes prefabricated and can hold one worker at a time, the scaffold must be created anew with each building so as to properly shadow its shape, and when complete, it can hold the weight of several crew members, all working together to accomplish a single task.

Now apply this metaphor to writing. Together, two or more writers "scaffold," creating a joint process that will hold them both as they work on the common task. Just like the construction scaffold, this one is built by several workers together and allows individual crew to go higher, reach further, than they could on a single ladder. And so the collaborative writers work with one another's "assistance that enables [them] to accomplish together what they can't do individually" (Burnett 128). In a collaboration, human nature assures us that there will be differences among the writers that will, in the end, allow the writers to accomplish together what they could not alone. By engaging one another's attention, interests, and feelings with a task and using shared expertise to fill in the gaps that one writer alone would have, writers complement one another and augment the quality of the single task (Bruffee "Writing and Reading" 161). Vygotsky first explained this concept in the context of children who, working with adults or with peers who are slightly more developmentally advanced, stretch beyond where they would go working alone. With adults who collaborate, it isn't that they are stretched to the edges of their development; rather, they are stretched to see ideas in different contexts and from different perspectives. Ultimately, both collaborative writers' views are stretched to a new place, one that, in order to accommodate both views, is different from the place that either writer alone would be. "Collaborwriters" Hal Blythe and Charlie Sweet describe how their minds work in this complementary way:

> If Charlie suggests what he considers an innocent line of dialogue, Hal, seeing it in a different light, might point out its lack of logic. [...] Even now, rereading this paragraph, we can't remember if Hal said this or Charlie said that; *we* said it all. [...] Maybe our collaborwriting isn't so much two heads but, as psychological studies are showing, an instance of being able to integrate Charlie's right brain and Hal's left brain. We're not saying that we're a pair of half-wits, but that we have complementary personalities. (42)

Blending the Voices

As a result of scaffolding, of writers working together to build a process and, in turn, create a piece of writing, the voices of the individual writers blend into a third. And this blended voice may be the most magical consequence of collaboration. Whether you chose to call this a blended voice, "third voice," "common voice," or "shared voice" (Alm 134), it is evidence that true collaboration occurs "when the product is so well integrated that it seems to be the creation of one mind" (Spooner and Yancey 52). This shared voice is evidence of synergy—the ability "to accomplish things together that neither [writer] could have accomplished alone"

(Reither and Vipond 858). As many collaborative writers attest, this new, synergistic voice can have power and presence much greater than either voice alone:

> Together we had a more powerful voice than each of us could muster individually. [...] Our two voices together [...] somehow could speak to audiences that might not have listened to either of us alone. [...] We remain in this [academic] world largely because that voice has been created in our collaboration [...] collaborating in our talky way allows—even insists on—a speech-like quality in the discourse that gets inside even our most academic prose. [...] As we write, we imagine [...] speaking [the text] together. And because we now theorize this double-voiced relationship consciously, we now recognize the process and the style that has come out of it as one strategy of resistance to the formal, impersonal, discourse and modes of the academy. (Ronald and Roskelly 256, 259)

Perhaps because they have experienced the creation of a distinct, blended voice, when collaborative writers return to solo writing, the voices of their coauthors are not silenced, but internalized. Each writer's style becomes more self-conscious because each has had the experience of becoming intimately familiar with another's voice and with blending that voice with his or her own. Moreover, this experience has left with each writer the voice of his or her coauthor, a voice that inspires confidence, that provides an ever-ready audience:

> Even when you're writing something alone, whether it's an article or another project or a memo or a committee report or whatever it is, it's easier. And I'm a very halting writer, and it's very easy for me to censor myself and say "I can't do this; I'm not doing this," and to get up and walk away. But the thing a writer needs is an audience who believes in you and to listen to what you have to say. Now, having written with Hepsie for all these years, she's in my head. And so, her voice, "Yes, you can do this. You're good. You're clever. You're smart," is right there next to that little editor that says, "You can't do this." And that, to me, is an amazing benefit of collaboration. (Ronald, Interview)

Pat Belanoff observes how her solo writing process and her style have been changed by overhearing her writing partner's voice inside her head:

> Our styles were really very different, and I certainly know that I have moved toward Peter's end of it. [...] I hear Peter's voice often. Particularly for me, when I'm working with a tangled sentence, and I realize that it's one of those things that in the past, I would have tried to develop some sort of complicated syntax to deal with the idea, and then I hear Peter's voice, and I realize that what I need to do is break it down. (Interview)

When writers make the move from solo to collaborative writing, then, they not only produce a written product that is greater or different from what each would have written alone; they also accrue enormous benefits when they return to writing solo. The habit of coauthoring allows writers to incorporate into their own repertoires the strategies of another writer.

Time for Reflection

Describe your writing process when you write alone. As an experienced writer, you probably have fixed writing strategies and habits. What rituals do you follow? What steps do you go through? Do you write with pen or pencil on paper or use the computer keyboard and screen? Try to imagine what habits you have as a solo writer that you'll have to change when you write with a partner.

Individual Changes for Individual Writers

In this chapter, we have outlined several changes that we believe to be necessary if one is to shift successfully from solo to collaborative writing. Starting with a paradigmatic ideological change, these changes also include changes in specific procedures and behaviors that occur throughout composing. While we don't feel at ease making an argument about changes necessary due to gender-defined characteristics, some researchers have done so. For example, collaborative writers and partners Kami Day and Michele Eodice argue extensively about the "feminine sensibility" that defines all collaboration (184). Citing Mary Lay, they maintain that "collaboration calls for a fundamental change in the self-image of men" (172). Certainly, collaborative writing experiences require coauthors to work in close physical, psychological, and intellectual proximity. The more they can do this with caring and respect, the greater their trust and the stronger their voice will be. Is this kind of working together something that is more difficult for men than women? If so, is this difference the result of cultural conditioning or genetic programming? Rather than try to answer these difficult questions, we ask you to look closely at your own ability to work with others in the manner necessary for a successful collaborative writing project. What kind of personal shifting from solo to collaborative writing will be necessary for you?

Trying Out Collaborative Writing

Based on shared interests or friendship, form writing teams of two or three in order to begin to work together on a writing project. It doesn't matter what the project entails, what its purpose is, or who its audience is. If you can't quickly think of a project, ask your instructor to "assign" one. Begin working on the project together by talking. After a period of sustained conversation to get the project underway, stop to consider together where the conversation has taken you. Are you ready to put words down on paper or up on a screen? To read or research? To give up on the project and start anew?

Talk about the talk, the turn-taking process you enacted. What connections can you make between your experience of moving from solo to collaborative composing and those you've read about in this and previous chapters? What differences can you notice? How effective was this attempt at writing together?

Works Cited

Alm, Mary. "The Role of Talk in the Writing Process of Intimate Collaboration." Ed. Peck and Mink 123–40.

Bishop, Wendy, and Hans Ostrom. E-mail. 27 September 2000.

Blythe, Hal, and Charlie Sweet. "Collaborwriting." *Writers on Writing.* Ed. Tom Waldrep. New York: Random House, 1985. 39–43.

Brodkey, Linda. "Modernism and the Scene(s) of Writing." *College English* 49 (1987): 396–418.

Bruffee, Kenneth. *Collaborative Learning: Higher Education, Interdependence, and the Authority of Knowledge.* Baltimore: The Johns Hopkins UP, 1993.

——. "Collaborative Learning and the 'Conversation of Mankind.'" *College English* 46.7 (November 1984): 635–52.

——. "Writing and Reading as Collaborative or Social Acts." *The Writer's Mind: Writing as a Mode of Thinking.* Ed. Janice N. Hays, et al. Urbana, IL: NCTE, 1983. 159–69.

Bruner, Jerome. "The Role of Dialogue in Language Acquisition." *The Child's Conception of Language.* Ed. A. Sinclair, R. J. Jarvella, and J. M. Levelt. New York: Springer-Verlag, 1978. 241–56.

Burnett, Rebecca E. "Decision-Making During the Collaborative Planning of Coauthors." *Hearing Ourselves Think: Cognitive Research in the College Writing Classroom.* Ed. Ann M. Penrose, and Barbara M. Sitko. New York: Oxford UP, 1993. 125–46.

Day, Kami, and Michele Eodice. *(First Person)²: A Study of Coauthoring in the Academy.* Logan: Utah State UP, 2001.

Elbow, Peter, and Pat Belanoff. *A Community of Writers: A Workshop Course in Writing.* 2nd ed. New York: McGraw-Hill, 1995.

———. Telephone Interview. 1 May 2000.

Knoblauch, Cy, and Lil Brannon. E-mail. 20 February 2001.

Lunsford, Andrea A., and Lisa Ede. *Singular Texts/Plural Authors: Perspectives on Collaborative Writing.* Carbondale: Southern Illinois UP, 1990.

Peck, Elizabeth G., and JoAnna Stephens Mink, eds. *Common Ground: Feminist Collaboration in the Academy.* Albany: State U of New York P, 1998.

Reither, James A., and Douglas Vipond. "Writing as Collaboration." *College English* 51.8 (December 1989): 855–67.

Ronald, Kate, and Hephzibah Roskelly. "Learning to Take it Personally." *Personal Effects: The Social Character of Scholarly Writing.* Ed. Deborah H. Holdstein, and David Bleich. Logan: Utah State UP, 2001. 253–66.

———. Personal Interview. 14 April 2000.

Spigelman, Candace. *Across Property Lines: Textual Ownership in Writing Groups.* Carbondale: Southern Illinois UP, 2000.

Yancey, Kathleen, and Michael Spooner. "A Single Good Mind: Collaboration, Cooperation, and the Writing Self." *College Composition and Communication* 49.1 (February 1998): 45–63.

For Further Reading

Dale, Helen. *Coauthoring in the Classroom: Creating an Environment for Effective Collaboration.* Urbana, IL: NCTE, 1997.

Forman, Janis, ed. *New Visions of Collaborative Writing.* Portsmouth, NH: Boynton/Cook, 1992.

Kleinmann, Susan. "The Reciprocal Relationship of Workplace Culture and Review." *Writing in the Workplace: New Research Perspectives.* Carbondale: Southern Illinois UP, 1993. 56–70.

Knox-Quinn, Carolyn. "Collaboration in the Writing Classroom: An Interview with Ken Kesey." *College Composition and Communication* 41.3 (October 1990): 309–17.

Lay, Mary M. "The Androgynous Collaborator: The Impact of Gender Studies on Collaboration." Ed. Forman 82–104.

Locker, Kitty O. "What Makes a Collaborative Writing Team Successful? A Case Study of Lawyers and Social Workers in a State Agency." Ed. Forman 37–62.

Rogers, Priscilla S., and Marjorie S. Horton. "Exploring the Value of Face-to-Face Collaborative Writing." Ed. Forman 120–46.

Selfe, Cynthia L. "Computer-Based Conversations and the Changing Nature of Collaboration." Ed. Forman 147–69.

Sharples, Mike, ed. *Computer Supported Collaborative Writing*. London: Springer-Verlag, 1993.

York, Lorraine. *Rethinking Women's Collaborative Writing*. Toronto: U of Toronto P, 2002.

CHAPTER

4

Let's Talk: What Is the Role of Conversation in Collaboration?

Lot of talk. LOTS of talk. Out loud brainstorming, a woman's conversation, many wandering diversions to create the wide beautiful track, lots of explaining our ideas and that touching off new ideas and coming around in a circle and laughing about not knowing what we were getting to or exactly where we had been. A long time the clock surprised us by saying it had been over three hours! The logical part of my brain saying at the end of that session: But have we gotten any farther than agreeing mostly on the ideas I came to her with three hours ago? Yes, we had, I believe: we had begun some new entity called Our Project. We had sparked ideas and validated thoughts and begun to shape something even though it still looked shapeless. Couldn't quantify it, but it was a learning process even if it didn't result in a paper right then to judge, or even a definite direction [. . .] During the second meeting, in the middle of us blabbing on about the paper, I heard myself stop and say, "Do you feel comfortable enough to tell me if you don't like an idea I come up with?" Andrea said yes, which I figured she would say, and I felt that way too. So then we plunged right in again to full speed brainstorming an thinking and discussing.
                    —Jana Zviebelman (qtd. in Elbow and Belanoff 75)

Writing is a technologically displaced form of conversation. [...]
Writing is at once two steps away from conversation and a return
to conversation. We converse; we internalize conversation
as thought, and they by writing, we re-immerse
conversation in its external, social medium.
—Kenneth Bruffee, "Collaborative Learning
and the 'Conversation of Mankind' " (641)

The two books we've worked on together both began in offhand
conversation about out lives and interests. The preface to each one
acknowledges the role of our talk in cultivating our ideas and
sustaining them through writing and more talk [...].
—Kate Ronald and Hephzibah Roskelly (256–67)

Personal Reflections on Conversation

During our more than fifteen years of collaboration, the two of us have joked about how apparently different we are from one another— the way we dress, our personal interests, our professional mannerisms, even our writing styles. At first meeting, neither one of us thought, "Ah ha! There's someone I can write with!" What did happen, as with many collaborative teams, is that through a progression of casual talk, shared observations and comments, and extended conversations, we became friends and, at the same time, came to see that although we were different in many ways, we shared many professional (and personal) perspectives and values. As we described in Chapter 2, during the first years of our friendship/collaboration, we were living in nearby towns, teaching at adjacent colleges in a consortium of five undergraduate colleges. Each of us was the only Composition specialist on her campus, and both were teaching in departments whose members were, at best, unconvinced of the value of our discipline. After initial conversations and brief exchanges at meetings or campus-wide events, walking out of a lecture hall, standing at the edge of a meeting room, we shared observations about a talk we had just heard or a meeting we had just attended. We knew of our common perspectives and felt confident of one another's discretion, and we moved our conversations to coffee houses or restaurants. What started out as talk about this or that faculty member or college decision soon grew into a shared interest about the way writing was taught at our consortium, who was being hired to teach it, and how useful it would be to write about our reflections. Our first collaborative project, and every one after that, has emerged from conversation. And as projects take shape, conversation continues to play a significant role throughout the creation of the piece—conversations to brainstorm ideas, determine the major conceptual organization of a piece, cast ideas for what we will write, reconsider sections of what we have written, or react to the other's words. Even though our collaborative habits have had to be adapted to our living on opposite sides of the country, conversation has remained the central, unchanging feature of our teamwork.

Not surprisingly, the nature of our conversations has changed with time and our own physical relocation. Once in a while we still enjoy the luxury of talking in the relaxed atmosphere of a college coffee shop or restaurant. More often, our conversations take place in airports, as we wait for our flights from conferences, in hotel lobbies or restaurants between conference sessions, over the phone in pre-arranged calls across time zones, or in e-mail exchanges that occur amid each person's respective daily activities. But, though their nature and pace have changed, the conversations continue to provide us an arena within which to discover our most current shared interests or concerns: "What did you think of the reviewer's comments about the essay we submitted?" "Do you have any graduate students doing administration in your department?" "How do you get your tutors to understand the difference between editing and tutoring?" "How do you use the portfolio in your M.A. program?" Questions like these come out of the small talk of two personally and professionally connected friends. Our "need" is to talk to someone we trust about something we've been thinking or feeling, about what has been bothering us or distracting our thinking. This particular need sometimes transforms into a larger one, to see how things we both feel or notice fit together. And it is in the fitting together that the first visible signs of a collaborative project begin.

Once our experiences and ideas have coalesced into a general idea, and we have agreed to devote time together to fleshing this idea into a conference proposal, a book, or an article, we almost always have a conversation about the title of whatever we are writing. These "title conversations" are critically important to the progress of the project. During this open discussion we exchange ideas, cast words, and propose and revise phrases, all of which provide us with the groundwork for the rest of our planning and writing. For it is in these discussions that we begin to generate what will, over time, become our shared creation. For example, the title of our second book, *Foregrounding Ethical Awareness in Composition and English Studies,* began as two separate lists of possible titles. Then, in a phone conversation that sounded like some esoteric television game show, we took turns reading our titles, back and forth, and when the lists were read, we identified individual words that seemed "right" to both of us; we built around those words, listened to the words, tried to see them on the cover of the book that was taking shape over the telephone lines between us. "Highlighting," "Noticing," "Observing," "Making Important"—these were all the words that were not quite the right words that we tested out on our way to "Foregrounding." "Awareness" was even more difficult to find among the other options that seemed to suggest something much more static and externally imposed than what we wanted. Interestingly, in this conversation about a project title, as in all of the others we have had, we didn't really know what we wanted—individually or together—until we had the conversation.

Although our conversations are most always important to germinating ideas, they are equally important throughout the writing process. For example, each time our projects reshape themselves from conference talks to articles to books, we have to return to the conversation that began with the first incarnation of the project. Several years ago, at a coffee shop in San Diego, unbothered by others around taking a break from the ongoing NCTE conference, we reshaped and developed an abstract for a book prospectus into a conference paper, knowing that this paper would, in the future, become the basis for an introduction to the book. The nature of our conversation was shaped by time constraints: not only would this be our only opportunity for face-to-face talk before the presentation, but the conference was only months away. Cups of coffee at our sides, we took a previously written text, and using pens (a laptop might have made it easier) we labeled what would be moved, added, deleted, and we jotted notes about the sections that each of us would continue to develop, hone, and improve. In the accompanying conversation, we asked how the other "saw" a particular section. Or we took turns casting out what the point of the whole piece "seemed to be." Once a question was posed or an idea floated, the remainder of the conversation was built from there—responses were suggested, ideas contemplated and reshaped, lines written and read aloud, notes to self recorded. After a couple of hours, we each packed up a well-marked copy of the initial text and left the coffee shop with a new shared vision of what the next incarnation of the project would be.

Conversation and Writing

In Chapter 1, we explained Vygotsky's idea that children's language development is both social and instrumental. In early language development, children speak aloud, as if to someone else, in order to figure out solutions to particularly difficult problems. Once language skills develop, the social basis of language internalizes, and children begin to engage themselves in silent conversations for the purposes of problem solving. By adulthood, individuals become so familiar with this process of internal conversation, that they are hardly aware they are doing it. It is only when faced with unexpectedly difficult situations that they revert to their early language behavior: They re-externalize the language that had become internalized, and they talk aloud. As the complexity of an action they engage in increases, so too does the role of speech in their problem-solving behavior (Bruffee "Writing and Reading" 165). We have all caught ourselves "talking aloud" when we get stuck figuring out a difficult problem or even sorting through the plans of an especially busy day.

The role that speech or conversation plays in the process of writing is twofold. First, writing is, by its very nature, a re-manifestation of talk. As Bruffee posits, "if thought is internalized public and social talk, then writing is internalized social talk made public again [...] if thought is internalized conversation, then writing is internalized conversation re-externalized" ("Collaborative Learning and the 'Conversation of Mankind'" 641). That is to say, what you think is an internalized response to the "conversations" you enter by listening or reading. The act of writing, both physically and cognitively, moves to the outside your internalized response to an ongoing conversation that you are now continuing. And so under any circumstances, writing is already a form of conversation.

Recalling, however, that humans use talk and conversation to help with complex problem solving, you need to consider the second role that speech plays in the writing process. For the solo writer, not only is the text-in-progress a conversation with herself and all the other voices in the "conversation of mankind" with which she engages, she may commonly use conversation with others to sort out rhetorical problems, determine the effectiveness of what she has written, figure out what she wants to write or what she has written. Many solitary writers need and use conversation with others in the course of writing. The purpose of this kind of conversation is to provide an external touchstone against which the writer can set her own evolving sense of the text she is writing. In both of these ways—as a defining feature of writing and as a tool the writer uses to draft and revise—conversation is a significant component in the generation of text.

Conversation in Collaborative Writing

As important as conversation with others is to solitary composing, it takes on a whole new role and even more tremendous value in the process of collaborative writing where the conversation is both immediate and ongoing. That is, in solo writing, writers engage in conversation by necessity as they enter the "conversation" that has preceded their writing, and writers may choose to reach out to other writers and readers for the conversation of feedback and response. But in collaborative writing, not only do the writers engage in the conversation with writers who have preceded them and solicit conversation as a response from others, once they make the decision to collaborate, they have committed themselves to a writing process that is rooted in conversation. While solo writing may include conversations with others, collaborative writing is "grounded in talk" (Alm 127). Ede and Lunsford characterize the relationship by explaining that "talk is central to our collaboration in a way that it seldom has been for us as individual writers" ("Collaboration and Compromise" 125). Those who write together firmly believe that "[c]onversation [...] is not a luxury, but a crucial element of collaboration" (Ashton-Jones qtd. in Alm 127). Indeed, every collaborative writer with whom we have spoken confirms what we have learned from our own collaborative writing experiences: that collaborative writing begins with conversation that continues throughout the writing process, changing purpose and format, but always needing to happen. Pat Belanoff describes the value of conversation as the foundation of her work with Peter Elbow:

> I was trying to think back to the whole thing of conversation, and it seems to me that obviously we talked all the time. But about the textbook, it wasn't necessarily that [the talk] was focused on the textbook as such. It's interesting—I think the conversation and talk was like the bedrock on which the book was built. (Interview)

In collaborative writing, conversation has a particularly fertile and generative power because it establishes the arena of negotiation and creation for the writers. In fact, it is **only** through conversation that writers working together can identify their shared concerns and shape their ideas. We think of our own experiences as friends who, through continued conversation, came to the point of collaboration. Another pair of coauthors whose books and articles are often cited in the field of Composition, Lil Brannon and Cy Knoblauch, have written to us about the important role conversation plays in their writing process: "We would say that talk in the early stages of conceptualization, and in between drafts of actual texts, is absolutely crucial. Indeed, it is the essence of our collaboration—because our writing habits couldn't be more different (in fact, they are virtually incompatible)" (E-mail).

The outside reader from whom both solo and collaborative writers solicit response has much less at stake than does the second or third writer in a collaborative writing set-up. Consequently, in collaborative writing the conversations are more thoroughly integrated throughout the whole process of writing; they are so well integrated, in fact, that, as for Knoblauch and Brannon, conversation becomes part of the definition of this kind of writing. For collaborating writers it would be next to impossible to separate conversation from writing. Recall Blythe and Sweet who arrange regular face-to-face conversations at the local fast food restaurant, creating a conversation schedule that is as predictable and inflexible as their teaching schedules. And knowing how critically important conversation would be to the progress of their work, Belenky and her colleagues made travel arrangements so that interruptions and physical distance would not impair the conversation the writers needed. Moreover, by agreeing to collaborate, the writers also implicitly agree that with their conversation "[they] are creating the optimum setting so that half-baked or emergent ideas can grow [...] [the conversation] reaches deep into the experience of each participant [...] [and] draws on the analytical abilities of each" (Belenky et al. qtd. in Alm 130). Ronald and Hephzibaz Roskelly write with great animation that for them, "collaboration remains primarily a matter of talk" (256):

> As with all the stages in our collaborative composing process, our jumbly drafting or invention is grounded in this kind of exploratory conversation. The talk quickly becomes a stimulant for as well as a record of our thinking. We not only begin to plan and draft the essay in our talk about it; we begin to shape how we'll talk about it. (260–61)

The collaborative writers are actually engaging in the externalization of the internal process of writing as they converse. While collaborative writers might use conversation in the conventional way that a solo writer does—to get response and feedback—they also use it to create their common ground, shuttling back and forth between/among themselves, offering, shaping, and reshaping the ideas that will become "theirs," reverting to this externalized form of language in the same way they first used it for problem solving. Gregory Clark explains that, "In essence, conversation is a cooperative endeavor sustained upon a foundation of shared meanings for the purpose of establishing further shared meanings that will support further cooperation and, thus further conversation" (37). And so conversation, oral language, becomes a tool by which ideas are created, meaning is negotiated, common threads are woven. Collaborative writers use conversation as a meaning-making tool and also as a means of facing an "old situation" (writing seemingly alone) in a new way (writing together).

The way conversation works in collaborative writing can also be thought of in relation to the concept of "scaffolding" that we have already described. As you may recall, psychologist Lev Vygotsky understands scaffolding to be part of the way humans function within the zone of proximal development. That is, when an individual works with someone whose capabilities or skills are just beyond his own, he will be able to piggy back on the skills of the other, creating a scaffold for himself that will allow him to work beyond the place where he could on his own. In the zone, individuals engage in "boundary discourse" (Bruffee *Collaborative Learning* 123), a kind of discourse that is used to understand the world at the very frontier of one's ability to understand it. Eventually, as he becomes more competent from practicing the skills, the scaffolding is "removed" and the individual works alone.

Now, apply this concept to a pair of collaborative writers. Rather than thinking in terms of skills, think in terms of knowledge or experience or perspective. What the two writers bring to the table is just different enough, one is just far enough out of reach of the other, that together they build a scaffold which reaches beyond and outside of where they would be working alone. For instance, when two people write together, the expertise that one might have in rhetorical criticism might fertilize the other's ideas on gender studies, pulling both of them along where each writer might not have gone on her own. That is, as Rebecca Burnett explains, "scaffolding enables writers to consider contextual and rhetorical elements that might not be considered otherwise" (129), to tap the expertise of a collaborator, filling in gaps, augmenting what we know, complementing our own thoughts and ideas (Bruffee "Writing and Reading" 161). This scaffold provides the framework that will hold the emerging ideas. Knoblauch and Brannon write about using talk to "get a feel for each other's position, take advantage of each other's arguments, insights, and exchange source materials from our different academic backgrounds, and steer each other out of impasses and away from intellectual blind spots" (E-mail). Referring more to the way personality difference can create sustaining "scaffolds" for fellow writers, Wendy Bishop explained that "[F]or a shy person [Hans] loaned me a supreme momentary self-confidence, or the playful 'what if' and 'why not' conversation did" (E-mail). Karen Burke LeFevre has described "resonance," as being "when an individual act of vibration is intensified or prolonged by sympathetic vibrations" (65). Collaborative writers provide this kind of resonance for one another as their conversation continues and sustains creative talk, prolonging the time of reaching closure and completion. Where the solo writer has only herself to convince that she has written enough on a subject or that all of the reader's questions have been answered, the collaborative writer must also convince the other writers engaged in the collaboration. The solo writer can stop asking for feedback and merely send the piece out for review, read it at a conference, or stick it in a drawer.

The collaborative writer always has another reader or readers to deal with, readers who are also writers invested in the value and effect of the product. Both or all of the writers must agree that the ideas in the text are resolved, enough has been said, the concepts are clear. Such agreement is often not quickly or easily reached. "What about [...]" "I just found an article that says [...]" "But in my department [...]" "I'm not sure I understand what you are saying on page [...]" And so, in collaborative writing, conversation pushes the generative moments of writing ever further out; it tests the synthetic strength of the text, tests until the synthesis is adequately complex and multidimensional to meet the critical force all the writers. Conversation continues until all writers are satisfied and a text exists that the solo writer could not have created.

Time for Reflection

Recall an especially difficult writing task that you accomplished. Write for a few minutes about how you tackled and completed that task, in particular, focus on the role that others played in the course of accomplishing the task.

The Nature of the Conversation

It can be helpful to think about conversation in a very practical sense as well, to identify and describe the qualities that different forms of conversation have and to define some very particular uses for conversation in collaborative writing. That is, although conversation is essential to collaborative writing, some qualities of a conversation can promote collaboration more than others. Furthermore, there are particular purposes for which conversation can be used that will be most likely to appear in the collaborative process. Using the term "dialogue" rather than "conversation," Paulo Freire identifies it as being "the encounter between men [sic], mediated by the world, in order to name the world" (76). In this way, Freire introduces dialogue as a very productive, action-resulting activity. Furthermore, dialogue is not "the act of one person's 'depositing' ideas into another, nor a simple exchange of ideas to be 'consumed' by discussion, nor is it a hostile, polemical argument between men, who are committed only to the imposition of their own truth" (77). Drawing on Freire's definition, then, if dialogue and conversation is going to be creative and productive, resulting in the action of idea-generation, the persons involved must respect one another and the process of dialogue/collaboration.

Consider, for example, Belenky and her collaborators. In writing *Women's Ways of Knowing*, they engaged in their own version of dialogue that they called "real talk," a kind of talk that "requires careful listening; it implies a mutually shared agreement that together you are creating the optimum setting so that half-baked or emergent ideas can grow. 'Real talk' reaches deep into the experience of each participant; it also draws on the analytical abilities of each" (qtd. in Alm 130). Another way to think about the mutual respect writing partners have for one another is in terms of the overall goal of the process—not for one to gain territory from another, but for both to arrive at a place they wouldn't have otherwise. Hans Ostrom describes this feeling in relation to his coauthor, Wendy Bishop, when he says, "We hardly ever argue or debate when we disagree because who cares who wins" (E-mail). The successful conversation between collaborators "advances the total sum of the discourse" (Bazerman qtd. in Clark 36), rather than the individual vision of any one writer.

In addition to being respectful and open, successful collaborative writing conversations seem to occur for one of four different purposes. Anne O'Meara and Nancy McKenzie's research shows that collaborating writers engage in (1) procedural talk that establishes working methods and deadlines; (2) substantive talk that centers on the content of the written products, like trying out sentences in one's head while writing alone; (3) writing talk that engages the writing team in a discussion of such elements as approach to drafting a paper, style and editing, format, and headings; or (4) social talk in which the writers chat about their personal and professional lives (212–14). You may be tempted to argue that these kinds of talk occur even among individuals engaged together in a hierarchical or cooperative writing task. While it's true that these talk topics or purposes may indeed be part of a cooperative writing activity, the "scene" in which they take place is not the same as for the collaborative writers who work together and believe, as we have already explained, that writing happens in the world, among others, and as such, manifests the social, meaning-making nature of language. Give and take, sharing and reacting, an interactive process characterizes each one of these categories of talk for the collaborative writers.

Writing partners don't necessarily engage in each of these types of talk for each project they work on together, especially if they have a long history of writing together. For instance, Knoblauch and Brannon describe their talk as predominantly, if not exclusively, "substantive," advancing the ideas of the piece they're writing together. They claim that, for them,

> talk in the early stages of conceptualization, and in between drafts of actual texts, is absolutely crucial. Indeed, it is the essence of our collaboration—because our writing habits couldn't be more different (in fact, they are virtually incompatible). Through talk, we get a feel for each other's positions, take advantage of each other's arguments and insights, exchange source materials from our different academic backgrounds, and steer each other out of impasses and away from intellectual blind spots. We absorb the results of this interplay before much writing actually takes place, knowing that the writing itself will necessarily depend more on one of us than the other and knowing that our ways of fashioning prose do not mesh well enough to allow for that more local kind of talk related to the tactics of organizing a text. (E-mail)

However, each of these kinds of talk is important to the collaborative process. In fact, even social talk, the kind that would seem least critical, enhances productivity by giving the writers motivation and commitment (215). When we write together, we find ourselves moving back and forth among these uses. Sometimes we make a phone call whose sole purpose is to set a deadline for the next phase of our work or even for the next extended conversation. The "title conversation" we described earlier is an example of one kind of substantive talk that we commonly have. Writing talk provides us with the kind of conceptual framework that allows us to work on shared projects from different regions of the country. And social talk runs alongside the whole process.

While collaborators use all of these kinds of talk, not all writers use them in the same way or not the same way in each instance of collaboration. Living thousands of miles apart, we simply don't have the opportunity for much sustained substantive talk. Blythe and Sweet, on the other hand, rely on substantive talk in which they literally co-write sections of their text at the table of their favorite fast food restaurant. And Knoblauch and Brannon, whose "writing habits couldn't be more different (in fact, they are virtually incompatible) [...] have never been able to sit down, pen in hand, and cooperate in drafting one sentence then the next" (E-mail). Instead, their conversations may be dominated by "writing talk" of the kind in which they "work mainly on the 'macro' level," working toward a shared "gist of the piece" (E-mail). And so, the way each pair or group of writers employs these four kinds of talk depends upon their own personal situations as well as their writing styles.

Trying Out Collaborative Writing

In pairs, share stories with one another about experiences you have had with collaborative projects, focusing particularly on the most and least successful. Extrapolating from those experiences, make two lists: the characteristics of successful collaboration and the characteristics of unsuccessful collaboration. Once you are done, recall specifically in what you write together next the generative value of the conversation in making the lists. What is your sense of how the conversation worked in the course of creating your two lists?

Works Cited

Alm, Mary. "The Role of Talk in the Writing Process of Intimate Collaboration." Peck and Mink 123–39.

Ashton-Jones, Evelyn, and Dene Kay Thomas. "Composition, Collaboration, and Women's Ways of Knowing: A Conversation with Mary Belenky." *(Interviews): Cross-Disciplinary Perspectives on Rhetoric and Literacy.* Ed. Gary A. Olson, and Irene Gale. Carbondale: Southern Illinois UP, 1991. 27–44.

Bishop, Wendy, and Hans Ostrom. E-mail. 27 September 2000.

Blythe, Hal, and Charlie Sweet. "Collaborwriting." *Writers on Writing.* Ed. Tom Waldrep. New York: Random House, 1985. 39–43.

Bruffee, Kenneth. *Collaborative Learning: Higher Education, Interdependence, and the Authority of Knowledge.* Baltimore: The Johns Hopkins UP, 1993.

——. "Collaborative Learning and the 'Conversation of Mankind.'" *College English* 46.7 (November 1984): 635–52.

——. "Writing and Reading as Collaborative or Social Acts." *The Writer's Mind: Writing as a Mode of Thinking.* Ed. Janice N. Hays, et al. Urbana, IL: NCTE, 1983. 159–69.

Burnett, Rebecca E. "Decision Making During the Collaborative Planning of Coauthors." *Hearing Ourselves Think: Cognitive Research in the College Writing Classroom.* Eds. Ann M. Penrose, and Barbara Sitko. NY: Oxford UP, 1993. 125–46.

Clark, Gregory. *Dialogue, Dialectic, and Conversation: A Social Perspective on the Function of Writing.* Carbondale: Southern Illinois UP, 1990.

Elbow, Peter, and Pat Belanoff. *A Community of Writers: A Workshop Course in Writing.* 2nd ed. New York: McGraw-Hill, 1995.

——. Telephone Interview. 1 May 2000.

Freire, Paulo. *Pedagogy of the Oppressed.* New York: Continuum, 1986.

Knoblauch, Cy, and Lil Brannon. E-mail. 20 February 2001.

LeFevre, Karen Burke. *Writing as a Social Act.* Carbondale: Southern Illinois UP, 1987.

Lunsford, Andrea A., and Lisa Ede. "Collaboration and Compromise: The Fine Art of Writing with a Friend." *Writers on Writing.* Volume II. Ed. Tom Waldrep. New York: Random House, 1988. 121–27.

O'Meara, Anne, and Nancy R. MacKenzie. "Reflections on Scholarly Collaboration." Peck and Mink 209–26.

Peck, Elizabeth G., and JoAnna Stephens Mink, eds. *Common Ground: Feminist Collaboration in the Academy.* Albany: State University of New York P, 1998.

Ronald, Kate, and Hephzibah Roskelly. "Learning to Take it Personally." *Personal Effects: The Social Character of Scholarly Writing.* Ed. Deborah H. Holdstein and David Bleich. Logan: Utah State UP, 2001. 253–66.

For Further Reading

Black, Laurel Johnson. *Between Talk and Teaching: Reconsidering the Writing Conference.* Logan: Utah State UP, 1998.

Cain, Mary Ann. *Revisioning Writers' Talk: Gender and Culture in Acts of Composing.* Albany: State U of New York P, 1995.

Calderonello, Alice Helm, Donna Beth Nelson, and Sue Carter Simmons. "An Interview with Andrea Lunsford and Lisa Ede: Collaboration as a Subversive Activity." *Writing on the Edge* 2.2 (1991): 7–18.

Dale, Helen. *CoAuthoring in the Classroom: Creating an Environment for Effective Collaboration.* Urbana, IL: NCTE, 1997.

Qualley, Donna J., and Elizabeth Chiseri-Strater. "Collaboration as Reflexive Dialogue: A Knowing 'Deeper than Reason.' " *Journal of Advanced Composition* 14.1 (1994): 111–30.

Roskelly, Hephzibah. *Breaking (into) the Circle: Group Work for Change in the English Classroom.* Portsmouth, NH: Heinemann Boynton/Cook, 2003.

York, Lorraine. *Rethinking Women's Collaborative Writing.* Toronto: U of Toronto P, 2002.

5

Can We Stop Yet? How Can Collaborative Writing Help Me Sustain Response and Delay Closure?

My other impulse is I don't explain. And that's why I don't go deep. I don't explain. And I sort of resent explaining. I want to just do a little story, and (let the reader) figure it out. [...] And so Kate has really helped me temper that impulse, made me kind of take time. Kate'll say, "OK, that's a good idea, but we have to do a little bit more here." And I'm like, "How much more?"
—Hephzibah Roskelly (Interview)

So we sent around drafts and we wrote all over them. [...] We said "Does that really make sense?" and "Say more," and "Why would you say that?" and "Where's your evidence?" [...]. If a work is embedded in a collaborative process, the writers goad each other into endless revisions. [...] in our study there's hardly a page that wasn't rewritten fifteen or twenty times. No one working alone can do that kind of intensive revision, nor can they benefit from the extensive redrafting that takes place in conversation. The kind of reflection and revising enabled by collaboration brings a quality of depth and scope to a work.
—Mary Field Belenky (qtd. in Ashton-Jones and Thomas 32)

When Do We Stop Writing?

I magine that you are at your computer keyboard working on a research paper assigned by your Advanced Composition instructor. Rereading the paper for the umpteenth time, you see that you have included everything you had planned to: The organization of the essay works to create and support your argument; the quotations are well integrated and documented. Overall, the paper just feels "right." But you still have two days before the paper is due. Is it finished? Do you ask a trusted reader to go over the paper for you and give you some feedback? Or do you set the paper aside, pulling it out once more before the deadline, rereading and revising a few more times before handing it in?

Now imagine you're working on a second paper, re-reading your words and feeling much more ill at ease. On the one hand, the paper is well edited—spelling and punctuation are perfect. It incorporates lots of correctly documented references to outside sources and includes all the major pieces of an essay: introduction, body, support, conclusion. But, on the other hand, some of the quotations you've included seem superfluous to the argument that you had intended to make, and some of the supportive arguments are not fully developed. You glance at the clock in the corner of the computer screen: The paper is due in 45 minutes, and you still have to drive to campus. Is the paper finished?

Time for Reflection

Recall a time in your writing history that is parallel to either of the scenarios above. Write out the story of what you did when the writing got done ahead of time or when the deadline arrived before you were ready. In either case, how did you feel about the writing? How important was the deadline to your sense of the writing's completion?

How do writers know when a piece of writing is "finished?" As students, you are used to pacing your writing according to deadlines. An instructor assigns a paper and provides a due date and time; barring extensions and incompletes, this is the point at which all drafting and revising is supposed to stop, and the "final copy" is turned in. But as the scenarios above suggest, a student's sense of when the writing is finished may or may not coincide with the instructor's deadline. Sometimes a deadline runs like an unnecessary stopwatch; sometimes it appears at the door like an ornery process server. In the latter case, the instructor's deadline doesn't so much determine when the *writing* is finished as it does determine when the *writer*, having run out of time, is finished.

But if imposed deadlines are excluded from the discussion, **then** how do writers know when to stop writing? To answer that, consider what happens when writers write. Drawing on the writing of phenomenological philosopher Eugene Gendlin, Sondra Perl explains that writers begin with a "felt sense," an emotional or physical sensation for what to do or say with a piece of writing. Whether the topic is assigned or self-selected, the process of writing begins, not with the writer's own written or spoken words, but with a pre-verbally motivated urge to express himself or herself in a particular way. Perl believes that when writers are cognizant of this felt sense, attentive to the inchoate level of meaning to which they must patiently ascribe the right words, they write much more "authentically" and honestly. Writers who exclaim, "I know what I want to say, but I'm just not saying it," are at this critical juncture between the non-verbal and verbal meaning. At this juncture, they may choose to be satisfied with what they have "said," and, not having found adequate linguistic expression, ignore or dismiss the emotional, physical source of expression. Or they can work to bring together the emotional and linguistic expression by using language to find language. That is to say, by having a conversation, talking to themselves, making an outline, list, freewrite, or cluster, they cast out words and sentences intended to represent the felt sense. The writer applies language to feeling to find the words that will most closely represent it, going back and forth between the words and the feeling, checking in and adjusting, asking whether the words fit, what has been left out or not fully expressed.

While this process of verbalizing the felt sense is already a complex, personal experience, it is complicated further by what we described to you earlier as the dialogic, public quality of language. According to Bakhtin because language is dialogic, every word is filled with the meanings of others who have used it, every idea a response to something the writer has heard or read or said. So, in the process we describe, writers are simultaneously drawing, weighing, and selecting from their own personal verbal pool the words that best represent their pre-verbal felt sense at the same time that they are checking and adjusting this selection against the meanings, voices, and conversation that are raised by their language. That is to say, writers are motivated by a need to respond both to the proximity between their available words and their felt sense ("This isn't the right word, but almost." "These sentences together seem to contradict each other." "What am I really trying to say here?") and to the past conversations that reverberate through the words ("Did Professor Cooper use the term in this way?" "But how can I answer the concerns raised in class?" "I remember discussing this concept with my writing group. What did they say?").

And this is what keeps writers writing, what keeps them from feeling as if a paper is finished. As long as there are responses to make to oneself, to a previous use of a word or an idea, as long as there is more language to find, and a felt sense to transform, the writing is unfinished.

Unfortunately, the "real world" or the writer's own choices can interfere with this write/respond/write process. Sometimes deadlines cut short this process, and sometimes the writer deliberately turns off the process, stopping the writing before it is finished. But theoretically, the writing continues and closure is delayed until all of the dialogue has been quieted, and the felt sense and the concrete language with all of its reverberations have overlapped, creating a single, focused image from the merging of others.

Time for Reflection

Reread the last Reflection that you wrote. In the margins of this writing, record responses you have to what you have written: questions that occur to you as an "outside" reader; comments or questions raised by other things you have read or heard; a conversation that your narrative initiates.

When Do Collaborative Writers Stop Writing?

So far, because it is the image of the writer most familiar to all of us, we have limited our description of the process of write/respond/write to the solitary writer. Of course, this process is extended when others are invited to be readers and the completion of the piece of writing is delayed, in this case, not by the writer's own self-generated response, but by questions and comments from a reader. And when the reader is also a collaborative writing partner, the write/response/write process is extended even further. As you've learned in Chapters 3 and 4, conversation is already a defining feature of collaboration. Consequently, questioning, commenting, and reacting are all built-in components of the collaborative composing process, providing the writer with "a person who both expands your thinking and comments on your thinking" (Roskelly, Interview). Unlike non-collaborating outside readers whose views are solicited when the writer chooses, collaborative writers respond to one another as a naturally and continually occurring part of the writing process. While the extent of the response may vary from being a relatively limited set of questions posed by a hierarchical collaborator to being a highly involved conversation with a dialogic collaborator, response is always a defining component of the writing process. And, whatever the extent of the collaborator's response, it is offered from a point of vested interest, of deep understanding and commitment to the writing.

So at the same time that the writer is internally responding to and negotiating the process of verbalizing a felt sense and creating meaning, a parallel response process is externalized as collaborative writers provide one another with the possibility of even more alternate meanings, competing voices, challenging questions, and ongoing conversation that will push the writing forward and delay the finishing of the piece. Speaking metaphorically of this process, Kate Ronald explains that "as a writer [Hepsie Roskelly], makes me go down side roads that I normally wouldn't go down, and she makes me look in odd places" (Interview). By prompting, adding information, challenging, and directing one another (Burnett 131), collaborative writers like Ronald and Roskelly look for what might be around the next blind corner, "make [one another] [...] take [her] time" (Interview), and, consequently, resist the urge to stop writing prematurely.

At this point, we are arguing, then, that all writing is powered by a process of responding to the accuracy, completeness, and aesthetic quality of what is being written. Writers, ideally, will keep writing as long as their response powers them in that direction. This naturally occurring process is multiplied several fold as outside readers are solicited and, further, when collaborative writers provide even greater catalysts for one another. Indeed, writers like Pat Belanoff who regularly collaborate not only come to appreciate the generative power that such response has for writing, but they find themselves seeking it even when they are not collaborating:

> [During one collaboration], I really felt like [Peter] was really taking it over and doing it; so I was really annoyed then, and I started to do some rewrite. I wanted to reclaim it back, I think; so I started to do a rewrite [...] but I also wanted to include what he wanted to do. And so I started out revising with most of those goals in mind, and what I realized, of course, is that most of the goals disappeared, and that somehow or another, I mean, that's one of the best lessons

in collaborative writing I've ever had. I somehow ended up with something that was not what I started with and not what he suggested, but it was just there. It was a much, much, much firmer unit and chapter [...] and I think that's what I got a real lesson on in collaborative writing [...] I don't write anything without showing it to somebody and asking them to look over it and see. And it doesn't have to be anybody in the field. Because I'm just looking to see some other things at that point, and sometimes somebody from the other side can really point out where you're off base. (Belanoff, Interview)

Should We Turn Off the Conflict?

What Belanoff discovers for herself about the value of seeking perspectives and ideas that conflict with her own is supported by Bruffee's theory about knowledge: "We establish knowledge or justify belief collaboratively by challenging each other's biases and presuppositions" (646). That is to say, without such challenges, knowledge stagnates. As a social instrument, then, language engages humans with one another, taps their individual expertise, and provides the blocks by which such expertise is shared, knocked down through disagreements, and rebuilt in new, often unexpected ways.

Referring to his work with Belanoff, Peter Elbow spoke with us about the importance that conflict or being "quarrelsome" had in their work: "The role Pat played back then was fairly often to be quarrelsome. And right from the beginning was very helpful and actually a relief to me [...] [I]t led to this feeling that when we collaborate, we don't have to agree. That each person can go where they're going, and that's not a problem; in fact, it's an advantage" (Interview).

However, not everyone is as inviting of conflict as Elbow and Belanoff. For at the same time that the conflict arising from comments and questions can be used to prolong and deepen the exploration and revision of some writers, it can also engender the kind of disagreements that many writers seek to avoid. And because it may be less uncomfortable or less difficult to ignore the conflicts that the writing raises than to figure out how to resolve them, writers may come to closure on a piece of writing prematurely. All writers are familiar with the experience of telling themselves that a draft "will do" or that the reader who pointed out some problems "just didn't get it." In instances such as these, writers are choosing the comfort of untroubled acceptance over the discomfort of disagreement.

Collaborative writers must make the same choice about whether to face or avoid conflict. During our research, we spoke with several individual writers who told us about times that they had chosen to avoid conflict and dissolve a collaborative endeavor. That is, the writers initially agreed to work together, began making plans, and may even have engaged in some writing, but at some point before the project was complete, the process broke down and the collaboration ended. Though we found that individuals in failed collaborations are often reluctant to elaborate on their experiences (generally out of kindness to one another), we do know that the failures are commonly caused by conflicts that the writers can't or don't know how to resolve. Ironically, although the central "function of collaboration is [for writers] to use language to induce cooperation in each other" (Klaris 114), the conflict that is necessary to motivate writing and delay premature closure also has the potential to undermine cooperation and collaboration altogether. If collaboration is to succeed, writers need to anticipate, understand, and accept this conflict. Ultimately, they need to use it to the advantage of their collaboration and the quality of their writing. But where do writers develop the tools to use conflict in this way?

Perhaps because teachers and researchers are, themselves, most familiar professionally with the negative, critical side of conflict (a point we will return to) in a well-intentioned effort to promote cooperation and goodwill among students, they often focus attention on ways to improve interpersonal skills, to foreground consensus and agreement. The results "can [...] prove [to be] dysfunctional" in ways the promoters certainly don't anticipate (Klaris 115). Students writing alone may all too easily avoid the conflicts that their own writing or outside readers raise to them, and collaborative writers may give up too easily on their belief, if not their participation, in collaboration. Klaris explains that in collaborative writing groups, a predetermined commitment to compromise "restricts and constrains the dialectical process which might permit the group members to discover or create the best possible solution" (116) and "restrict the invention process" (121). This is not to say that compromise and cooperation are not important and necessary features of collaborative writing. Rather, they may not be best positioned as the primary features of the process, ahead of the give and take, agreement and disagreement, sharing and shaping that characterize dialogue. Putting compromise and cooperation first, writers may come to closure and "finish" a piece of writing well before it has had the opportunity to mature beyond the state of its initial germination.

Time for Reflection

Remember a time when you were part of a collaboration that fell apart and never completed its intended project. You needn't restrict your recollection to writing experiences—it could be any kind of experience where you were working with one or more individuals. Write about how the collaboration began, and then trace what happened as it came to its end.

All Conflicts Are Not Equal

If collaborative writers are to use conflict to their own benefit, they must first recognize that not all conflict is equal. Writers must determine which conflicts to pursue and which to give limited attention to, distinguishing those conflicts which have the potential to ignite destructive hostility from those conflicts in which a non-aggressive reexamination of ideas is likely to occur as participants enter one another's perspectives.

Indeed, the success or failure of a collaboration can hinge on writers knowing which conflicts should receive attention and which ones shouldn't. Recalling the topics of conversation that Burnett described, research indicates that affective conflicts emerging from personal disagreements among the authors or procedural conflicts that focus on the practices writers use in order to work together are not nearly as valuable or productive as substantive conflicts that focus writers' attention on alternative ideas and the goal of reaching stasis (Burnett 133). Given the nature of collaboration, personal disagreements and procedural conflicts are expected and must be resolved through respectful discussion, but if writers can't get beyond these conflicts, and they dominate the writers' relationship at the expense or even the exclusion of substantive conflict, they may also derail the writing process altogether.

As we have said, the subject of substantive conflict is the content of the writing itself. Such conflict engages writers in an exchange of questions, reactions, and comments and extends the time writers speculate on and shape ideas, and, consequently, defers consensus and delays the "finishing" of a piece of writing. Substantive conflict gives "collaborators time to generate and critically examine alternatives and voice disagreements on their way to making discoveries" (Burnett 146).

Time for Reflection

Thinking again about the collaboration that ended before its project was finished, how would you characterize the kinds of conflict that occurred? Were they most like personal, procedural, or substantive conflicts? In retrospect, how do you think they were responsible for the end of the collaboration? Could this untimely end have been avoided?

Learning to Believe

Substantive conflict requires that writers take the time to hear and try out one another's ideas, to play with and alter them, to reject and re-select. Without such time, the chances are greater that one individual's ideas will uncritically dominate, that the richness that comes from the blending and shaping of different ideas will be pre-empted and lost. Writers must see and sustain conflicts between and among the *ideas* they hold and, in turn, use such differences for generative, revisionary purposes. Writers who allow themselves to step into and see other perspectives can then return to their own perspectives and use the recently visited one as a way to improve on the familiar. The conflict that interests us in the collaborative writing process emerges, then, not from one or more individuals attacking others' perspectives and promoting his or her own as the preferred one, but from individuals placing one or more perspectives side by side, opening themselves to other perspectives, and then letting the natural conflict and evolution of ideas occur. Unfortunately, many of us are relatively unpracticed in this more generative, affirming use of conflict, a fault that may, in fact, influence the nature, if not the caliber, of our work.

Relating the way we engage in intellectual conflict directly with the quality of thinking that occurs, Elbow argues that "we can improve our understanding of careful thinking or reasoned inquiry (and thereby improve our practice) if we see it as involving two central ingredients": the believing game and the doubting game (*Embracing Contraries* 255). As academics, we are most familiar with the act of doubting: "[w]e tend to assume that the ability to criticize a claim we disagree with counts as more serious intellectual work than the ability to enter into it and temporarily assent" (258). What we miss by restricting ourselves to the confrontational posture whose purpose is to identify dissonance and reject unfamiliar ideas (264) is the opportunity to enter fully and adequately into another perspective for the purpose of accumulating a set of intellectual building blocks that can be used to reshape and strengthen our own thinking. Indeed, though we tend to engage in such doubting as the dominant or even the sole means to intellectual advancement, Elbow argues that "the best way to get out of one's original frame of reference is [not by criticizing and doubting, but] by playing the believing game with some very different ideas—ideas which at first may appear odd or threatening" (*Everyone Can Write* 78).

Certainly Elbow's use of the term "game" belies the seriousness of the enterprise he is promoting, one that he identifies as being both "methodological" and "disciplined" (*Embracing Contraries* 260), a conscious, willful choice on the part of participants. Using the reading of literary texts as his example, Elbow explains that "[w]hat makes this process different from most academic inquiry is that we are not trying to construct or defend an argument but rather to transmit an experience, enlarge a vision" (261). In a similar way, what distinguishes our view of conflict in collaboration is that it does not ask writers to criticize and reflexively reject their coauthor's perspective, but rather to improve their own thinking by entering willfully into this other perspective.

Not only can reflexive doubting severely limit the depth and breadth of the ideas one can develop, its defensive, uncompromising posture poses potential harm to collaboration. It is through the act of believing, of entering into the alternate or different perspective so as to build between or among them a richer, more unexpected one, that community among the writers is created (*Embracing Contraries* 264). So at the same time that such activity discourages writers from finishing a piece too soon and not exploring unanticipated and potentially valuable avenues of thought, it also helps to strengthen the collaborative team itself.

Trying out Collaborative Writing

Now we'll give you a chance to try out the collaborative process of believing and doubting. Once you have read the following quotation, write a half-page response in which you state your own reaction to its "truth."

"We have suggested that it is useful to think of writing and knowing as profoundly collaborative processes. We have thus argued for a re-visioning of collaboration to include not only coauthoring and workshopping, but also knowledge making. All of us who write must ground our language in the knowing of those who have preceded us. We make our meanings not alone, but in relation to others' meanings, which we come to know through reading, talk, and writing" (Reither and Vipond 862).

Pair up with someone else in your class, and first, engage in the process of listing all of the reasons you can think of that would make this quotation true. Next, engage in the opposing process, doubting this same quote and listing all the reasons why this is not a true perspective. Once you are done, return to what you originally wrote about the quotation and write once more, this time about the way in which engaging in these two processes influenced the perspective with which you began.

Works Cited

Ashton-Jones, Evelyn, and Dene Kay Thomas. "Composition, Collaboration, and Women's Ways of Knowing: A Conversation with Mary Belenky." *(Interviews): Cross-Disciplinary Perspectives on Rhetoric and Literacy.* Ed. Gary A. Olson, and Irene Gale. Carbondale: Southern Illinois UP, 1991. 27–44.

Bruffee, Kenneth. "Collaborative Learning and 'The Conversation of Mankind.'" *College English* 46.7 (November 1984): 635–52.

Burnett, Rebecca. "Conflict and Consensus in Collaborative Decision-Making." *Professional Communication: The Social Perspective.* Ed. Nancy R. Blyler and Charlotte Thralls. Newbury Park, CA: Sage, 1993. 144–62.

Elbow, Peter. *Embracing Contraries: Explorations in Learning and Teaching.* New York: Oxford UP, 1986.

——. *Everyone Can Write: Essays Towards a Hopeful Theory of Writing and Teaching Writing.* New York: Oxford UP, 2000.

Elbow, Peter, and Pat Belanoff. Telephone Interview. 1 May 2000.

Gendlin, Eugene T. *Experiencing and the Creation of Meaning.* New York: Free P, 1962.

Klaris, Bill. "Conflict in Collaboration." *Rhetoric Review* 8 (1989): 113–26.

Perl, Sondra. "Understanding Composing." *College Composition and Communication* 31.4 (December 1980): 363–69.

Reither, James, and Douglas Vipond. "Writing as Collaboration." *College English* 51.8 (December 1989): 855–67.

Ronald, Kate, and Hephzibah Roskelly. Personal Interview. 14 April 2000.

For Further Reading

Cross, Geoffrey A. *Collaboration and Conflict: A Contextual Exploration of Group Writing and Positive Emphasis.* Cresskill, NJ: Hampton P, 1994.

Flores, Christopher. "Collaboration in Conflict: What Happens When Two Scholars Work Together on a Project—and Things go Horribly Wrong?" *The Chronicle of Higher Education* 14 (June 2002): A14–16.

Janangelo, Joseph. "Carnage and Response: Reconceiving Gaming Strategies in Our Professional Dialogues." *Dialogue* 2.1 (Spring 1995): 6–22.

Locker, Kitty O. "What Makes a Collaborative Writing Team Successful? A Case Study of Lawyers and Social Workers in a State Agency." *New Visions of Collaborative Writing.* Ed. Janis Forman. Portsmouth, NH: Heinemann Boynton/Cook, 1992.

Podis, Leonard A., and JoAnne M. Podis. "Opinion: The Rhetoric of Reproof." *College English* 63.2 (November 2000): 214–28.

Trimbur, John. "Consensus and Difference in Collaborative Learning." *College English* 51 (1989): 602–16.

6

Losing My Identity: How Do I "Co"mingle in "Co"authorship?

When it came time to turn our manuscript over to the publisher, we anguished over how we could communicate the truly collaborative nature of our work in a linear culture that insists the order of authorship as indicating the degree of contribution. The only solution (since the publisher did not think a circle of names would work) was to arrange our names alphabetically. Even so, "Belenky" became known to many as the author; the rest of us often disappeared into the "et al."

—Nancy Rule Goldberger (qtd. in John-Steiner 144)

When we first began our collaborative journal [...] we debated whether or not to keep "tracings" of our individual contributions. We discovered that as our collaboration progressed, it became increasingly difficult to see who wrote what because the combination of reading, writing, and conversing—especially on the fluid medium of the word processor—erased discourse boundaries, erased ownership, and foregrounded the practical negotiations involved in creating a collective text.

—Chris Anson, Laura Brady, and Marion Larson (87)

We often lost track of who started something and who "owned"
a section or an idea. We pretty much drifted or fell into this
method: we were in a hurry, we knew we had a lot to write,
and we didn't have time or energy to "protect" everything
we wrote. Most of all we trusted each other.

—Pat Belanoff (qtd. in Elbow and Belanoff SR-32)

When Does It Mean to Want to "Own" a Piece of Writing?

Recall the first time you got feedback to your writing from a tutor in the campus writing center or from a writing instructor in her office. Did you feel possessive or defensive about your words and ideas when you heard the tutor's questions about your paper, even if it was only a rough draft? Did you respond differently when a writing teacher asked a question about meaning, rewrote a sentence, or had a problem with word choice or phrasing in one of your papers and suggested her revision? And what do you remember about your first experience with peer groups in a writing class? Did you hold back on giving a critical response to someone else's paper? Did you avoid dealing with a response from a peer that might cause you to have to add something new to your paper? Did you instinctively immediately respond to comments from your peer group by defending "your" ideas expressed in "your" words?

When you were first required to share your writing with tutors in the writing center, with peers in class, or even with your writing instructor, you may have resisted suggestions for revision or the editorial hand of the writing instructor because you thought that only you knew what you were trying to say in your writing and that your writing should be your very own ideas and words, unadulterated by the influence of others. You may have exerted textual ownership, that is, wanting to have some say or control over what a text means and control over the language that makes its meaning. Like Edward, a student in Candace Spigelman's study of textual ownership in student writing groups, you may have needed to claim: "I am the owner of my essay. It was completely mine, thought by me and written by me. [...]" (*Across Property Lines* 70).

On the other hand, at times perhaps you've found it *too* easy to relinquish control and ownership of your writing when you're faced with certain kinds of responses from readers. Maybe you found comments on a paper, whether from a peer or a teacher, daunting, uncontestable. It's as if you were intimidated by the authorial ethos of the reader's comments in print and couldn't think of a "better" way to say it, couldn't get the reader's words out of your head. Or maybe the reader had hit upon exactly what you wanted to say and expressed your meaning more clearly and deftly than you had. In the process of responding to one of these types of review, you may have decided to incorporate in your paper ideas, words, a metaphor, a turn of phrase that the reader/reviewer/evaluator used in his or her comments/responses/suggestions for revision.

In addition to your concern about losing control of your text, you may also have allowed concerns about plagiarism and intellectual property to interfere with your taking the advice of your readers. You may have heard inside your head the voices of writing teachers from the past reminding you to aspire to produce an original text and to avoid plagiarism. Composition scholar Rebecca Moore Howard observes that this anxiety about control, ownership, and originality derives from an "economy of authorship in which only the writer who can work alone, autonomously, free of others' influence, can produce 'original' text" (479). This anxiety derives from a belief that writing is a solitary act uninfluenced by what others have written and persists despite the fact that, as Howard notes, and as we have argued from the very beginning of this book, "Contemporary theory rejects the possibility of original, uninfluenced writing and even the possibility of fully acknowledging one's sources" (474). In fact, the Russian literary critic Mikhail Bakhtin, whom we referred to in Chapter 1, claimed that "Quests for my own word are quests for a word that is not my own." If that is the case, "then how can we ever assign responsibility for the acts that words are?"—or authorship (Clark and Holquist qtd. in Lunsford and Ede *Singular Texts/Plural Authors* 92).

If some of these scenarios describe your past experiences with readers' feedback, you are not alone in feeling the continual pull of wanting to "own" your writing rather than surrender control of it to your readers. In fact, when Spigelman set out to study the attitudes toward authorship that first-year writers brought to writing groups, she found what she termed "cultural 'habits of mind' " about textual ownership, authorship, and intellectual property that they'd acquired by living and being educated within a Western worldview where written text is considered the work of an individual's labor to be protected by copyright ("Habits of Mind" 234). Spigelman found in her case study of a four-member college-level writing group that when the group met in their composition classroom, participants were torn between the image of the writer who writes alone and the writer who shares the labor with other writers: "At times, they invoked a discourse of shared labor to talk about their contributions to the making of meaning in their peer's essays. At other moments, their discursive constructions undermined notions of multiple-authorship and refocused on the individually-authored and individually-owned text" ("Habits of Mind" 241).

Time for Reflection

From one or more of the following—(1) a peer review session, (2) a tutoring session in the writing center; and (3) comments from a teacher on one of your rough drafts—write about some tensions that you remember feeling about how the words and ideas in a paper you were working on did and did not "belong" to you. How did you resolve those tensions? What do you think were the sources of those tensions for you?

How Do Collaborative Writers Deal with Questions of Textual Ownership?

A second case study of a five-member creative writing group meeting monthly at a local coffee bar provided Spigelman with a different take on the dialectical process of private and public textual production. And, for our purposes in this book, the committed writers in this self-sponsored group preview the ways collaborative writers deal productively with the concomitant needs to own text individually and jointly. Unlike the novice writers in the composition classroom, the writers in this working writers' group were more than willing to share temporarily ownership of one another's texts in "an economy of exchange and reciprocity" that is not unlike the kind of transaction writers seek to foster when they decide to write collaboratively. Spigelman's description of the features of this writing group could be a description of collaborative writing partners:

> Convinced that textual production is inherently intertextual and collabora-tive, [these writers] seek suggestions from their peer readers. Motivated by the prospect of complementary transaction, they freely assume partial ownership of the texts they read, placing themselves in the role of "writer." From the synergy of their engagement, members' words and interpretations "interanimate" each other, creating new readings and writings. (*Across Property Lines* 69)

All the advice about writing groups tells you to retain control—ownership—of your work. It's always ultimately your paper, so you don't have to change it as a peer reader or tutor suggests you should. The individual author is always right. But in truly collaborative writing, this cannot be the case ever. Such feedback causes response; like writing, response from readers generates more, better writing. To write collaboratively, you have to understand, as we argued in Chapter 1, that knowledge is constructed by writers and talkers together and in groups. The responding to your writing in talk, on paper, and online that goes on in writing centers, writing groups, and writing classrooms enacts this view of knowledge-making, no matter whether the work in progress is ultimately attributed in published form to a single author or to multiple authors. But the ideology of the writer who writes alone and the importance of individual achievement regularly interfere with dialogic collaboration. What is it, then, that can motivate writers to allow their own textual ownership to be less important than the meaning and rhetorical effect of a finished piece of writing? When writers decide to write collaboratively, these concerns about textual ownership do not suddenly disappear. You'll see that, just as novice writers who carry the image of the writer who writes alone in their minds, coauthors worry about individual status and ownership. But writers who have decided to write together are motivated to make these concerns part of the reflective negotiation that, as you have learned in Chapters 4 and 5, characterizes a dialogic collaborative writing process.

Several teams of collaborative authors write about their concerns and the ensuing negotiations. Expressing reservations about feeling "coerced toward consensus," Chris Anson, Laura Brady, and Marior Larson have trouble deciding what belongs to "we" in their writing process and whether all the "I's" will need to be subsumed into the "we" of consensus (85). The conflict between individual authority and group consensus bothers Virginia Monseau, Leanne Gerlach, and Lisa McClure as they wanted to collaborate on their book as editors while they "retain [their] individual voices" (65). Kathleen Yancey and Michael Spooner resist consensus altogether at times when they truly disagree. They note that their "disagreement makes the blender-voice of many coauthored pieces virtually impossible for this one. Besides the disagreement is part of the content. It's important to show that while we do work toward each other, we finish feeling that there is still room for two separate soapboxes at the end. At least two" (253). In the manner of hierarchical collaboration, Stephen Fishman and Lucille McCarthy take credit for individual chapters in their book *John Dewey and the Challenge of Classroom Practice* and indicate first and second authorship on chapters that are coauthored. As Ronald and Roskelly observe about this practice of dividing up the work, "This convention is an acknowledgment of a method of collaboration that doesn't risk a loss of individual autonomy or threaten academic, literary, and cultural models of individual achievement and accountability. [. . .] The two writers are in dialogue with one another and with their subject, but they retain their own selves as they write" (265).

Even writers who work ultimately toward a blended third voice may decide to delay effacing the individual voice; they postpone the writing over or voice-merging. For example, Mary Field Belenky recalls how the authors of *Women's Ways of Knowing* intentionally retained personal ownership and individual voices by sending hard copies of text to one another with comments written in the margins because "If you send your disk around and people start changing it, your words and theirs get merged too fast." As part of their collaborative process, Belenky, Goldberger, Clinchy, and Tarule decided to "keep all of the different voices separate for awhile" (Ashton-Jones and Thomas 32). Interestingly, even when speaking of the ultimate merging of the four voices, Belenky does so in terms of ownership:

> Sometimes I found myself [. . .] integrating into my own text a beautiful perception from someone else's text, their words and my words. [. . .] It's so loving to have that mingling going on—knowing that these are stolen words in a way, words coaxed out of someone, but liking the closeness of having her words and my words all mingling right in there. (Ashton-Jones and Thomas 32)

Others who choose to write collaboratively have less concern about letting go, losing control of the individual voice, during any part of the process. In shifting to *"we* need to" from "I think *you* need to," Ronald and Roskelly conclude "that the 'we' being created is more important than the 'I' that we're letting go" (262–63).

Time for Reflection

Is there anything in your past writing experience that prepares you to "disappear into the 'et al.' " as Goldberger, Clinchy, and Tarule did, or to "erase ownership" as Anson, Brady, and Larson chose to do? Write briefly about this question, and share your reflections with a potential writing partner.

Representing "Plural Authors" of "Singular Texts"

In figuring out how to represent the co-mingling, the blended voice of truly dialogic collaborative writing to external audiences or reviewers, coauthors have come up with printed and visual representations that show the co-mingling in pragmatic, theoretical, metaphorical, sometimes even playful ways. These graphical and rhetorical moves are intended to show the reader/the audience/the reviewer how the coauthors conceive of their merged identities. For instance, years ago at the most pragmatic, mundane level, from the start of our collaborative partnership, we rather naïvely decided to list our names alphabetically for our presentations and publications, and we have not deviated from that position. That initial decision caused us not to have to reconsider every time we coauthored something about whose name would be listed first. Looking back on it now, we realize, although we didn't know it at the time, that that decision may have helped us move rapidly into a dialogic mode of writing together and adopt a sense of "co" ownership of our words. This decision led us to another important practice that we've been enacting throughout the writing of this book: Much as Ronald and Roskelly did in establishing their collaborative voice, "we quickly realized that, to avoid confusion, the only 'we' that could ever appear in our work together had to refer only to us—[Sheryl and Susan]—not to teachers in general, the profession, or humanity" (262).

Ede and Lunsford made what was perhaps a more informed decision to alternate the order of their names: On the one hand, they admit to feeling "less ego involvement with our coauthored essays" and "more willing to loosen our proprietary connection or hold on our 'own' words. This latter point may be reflected in the care with which we alternate our names as first authors—we thought that listing our names alphabetically would indicate that we were equal collaborators, but were quickly disabused of that notion [...]" ("Collaboration and Compromise" 126). The husband-and-wife team of Composition scholars Cy Knoblauch and Lil Brannon explain that their initial decision to become "Knoblauch and Brannon" was based on technological changes. According to Brannon, "When we first started writing together, we decided whose name would go first by who typed the final draft. After our first book, we bought our first computer together. The drudgery of typing did not work then for placing our names on articles. I'm not sure now how we decided to go with Knoblauch and Brannon, but at some point we thought it best just to stick with one way of referring to ourselves" (E-mail). Some of the teams whom Day and Eodice interviewed for their study of coauthoring in the academy reported a "nurturing stance" toward solving the first author/second author dilemma: They asked " 'Who needs to be first author?' " (67). This attitude takes into account the hierarchical methods of evaluation that prevail in the academy that Ede and Lunsford refer to above.

Trying to capture with linear text the non-linear process of co-mingling, or what Ronald and Roskelly refer to as the "doubled presence" (256) or the running-together of names, has resulted in some interesting rhetorical and visual strategies. One time-honored method of representing the blended voice is the pseudonym, borrowed by academics from the world of commercial creative writing, for example, Claire Munnings for academic administrators Jill Ker Conway and Elizabeth Kennan when they're writing mysteries together (Whitcomb 118), or Hal Charles, a collaborative pseudonym for literature professors Hal Blythe and Charlie Sweet (42). Lisa Ede and Andrea Lunsford toyed with the idea of combining their names as Annalisa Edesford to represent their collaborating voice. Michael Spooner explains how he and Kathleen Yancey came up with their collaborative pseudonym, Myka Vielstimmig: "Myka is a sort of Russian-sounding jumble of a few letters from our two names. Vielstimmig is a legit word in German for 'multivocal'" (Day and Eodice 118n6). In addition, in three coauthored articles, Yancey and Spooner used different fonts and spacing on the printed page to try to capture graphically for readers the back-and-forth process of their e-mail conversations and to represent the "multivocal" quality of their collaborative voice ("Concluding the Text," "Postings," "A Single Good Mind").

Some of the print strategies collaborative partners have devised are theoretically and metaphorically driven. For example, the front cover design of *Singular Texts/Plural Authors* creates what might be called in computer lingo "wallpaper" with the continual repetition of coauthors' names underneath the title: [...] Andrea Lunsford Lisa Ede Andrea Lunsford Lisa Ede Andrea Lunsford Lisa Ede [...] The cover, then, is the graphical representation of shared ownership, the equal co-mingling of the partners. The message to readers is that there is no first author or second author. Day and Eodice report on an intriguing design used on the title pages of a coauthored dissertation and a coauthored scholarly book that employs a circular icon as a type of logo that makes a circle out of the two coauthors' names (46n9). For their coauthored book, Day and Eodice borrowed the mathematical signifier for exponential growth for their title (*First Person*)[2], to indicate "that knowledge, insight, productivity, rhetorical sensitivity, creativity, the ability to find common ground through negotiation, appreciation of the strengths of others [...] have the potential to grow exponentially when people write together" (82–83). All these graphical signifiers point unequivocally and visibly to shared ownership of text.

Perhaps the most unexpected and ultimate erasure of ownership that collaborative writers can learn from comes not from the work of authors, but from a pair of twentieth century painters. Psychologist Vera John-Steiner's description of the way in which Picasso and Braque, the creators of Cubism, renounced personal ownership in favor of the collaborative transformation of their art provides a telling close to this chapter:

> At one point in their collaboration, each signed his own name, not in front, but on the back of the canvas: in this way the painter's identity remained in the background. "We were inclined to efface our personalities in order to find originality," Braque wrote. And Picasso recollected: "So you see how closely we worked together. At that time our work was a kind of laboratory research from which every pretension or individual vanity was excluded." (John-Steiner 68)

Trying Out Collaborative Writing

Pair up with a writing partner to put down on paper or up on the screen some reactions to these decisions about how to represent dialogic collaborative writing. Every few phrases or sentences, stop to reread the text you are generating. On a separate piece of paper or a split screen, make two columns, one for each of you, and place the words or phrases or sentences that "belong" to each of you in the appropriate column. Discuss what you're observing about writing collaboratively from this exercise.

Works Cited

Anson, Chris, Laura Brady, and Marion Larson. "Collaboration in Practice." *Writing on the Edge* 4.2 (Spring 1993): 80–96.

Ashton-Jones, Evelyn, and Dene Kay Thomas. "Composition, Collaboration, and Women's Ways of Knowing: A Conversation with Mary Belenky." *(Interviews): Cross-Disciplinary Perspectives on Rhetoric and Literacy.* Ed. Gary A. Olson, and Irene Gale. Carbondale: Southern Illinois UP, 1991. 28–44.

Blythe, Hal, and Charlie Sweet. "Collaborwriting." *Writers on Writing.* Ed. Tom Waldrep. New York: Random House, 1985. 39–43.

Day, Kami, and Michele Eodice. *(First Person)²: A Study of Coauthoring in the Academy.* Logan: Utah State UP, 2001.

Elbow, Peter, and Pat Belanoff. *Sharing and Responding Booklet. A Community of Writers: A Workshop Course in Writing.* New York: McGraw-Hill, 1989.

Howard, Rebecca Moore. "Sexuality, Textuality: The Cultural Work of Plagiarism." *College English* 62.4 (March 2000): 473–91.

John-Steiner, Vera. *Creative Collaboration.* New York and London: Oxford UP, 2000.

Knoblauch, Cy, and Lil Brannon. E-mail. 20 February 2001.

Lunsford, Andrea, and Lisa Ede. "Collaboration and Compromise." *Writers on Writing.* Volume II. Ed. Tom Waldrep. New York: Random House, 1988. 121–27.

——. *Singular Texts/Plural Authors: Perspectives on Collaborative Writing.* Carbondale, IL: Southern Illinois University Press, 1992.

Monseau, Virginia R., Jeanne M. Gerlach, and Lisa J. McClure. "The Making of a Book: A Collaboration of Writing, Responding, and Revising." *Writing With: New Directions in Collaborative Teaching, Learning, and Research.* Ed. Sally Barr Reagan, Thomas Fox, and David Bleich. Albany: State U of New York P, 1994. 61–75.

Ronald, Kate, and Hephzibah Roskelly. "Learning to Take It Personally." *Personal Effects: The Social Character of Scholarly Writing.* Ed. Deborah H. Holdstein, and David Bleich. Logan: Utah State UP, 2001. 253–66.

Spigelman, Candace. *Across Property Lines: Textual Ownership in Writing Groups.* Carbondale: Southern Illinois UP, 2000.

——. "Habits of Mind: Historical Configurations of Textual Ownership in Peer Writing Groups." *College Composition and Communication* 49.2 (May 1998): 234–55.

Whitcom, Clare. "Jill Ker Conway and Elizabeth Kennan: Partners in Crime." *Victoria* (May 2001): 118–19.

Yancey, Kathleen Blake, and Michael Spooner. "Concluding the Text: Notes toward a Theory and the Practice of Voice." *Voices on Voice: Perspectives, Definitions, Inquiry.* Ed. Kathleen Blake Yancey. Urbana, IL: NCTE, 1994. 298–314.

———. "Postings on a Genre of Email." *College Composition and Communication* 47.2 (May 1996): 252–78.
———. "A Single Good Mind: Collaboration, Cooperation, and the Writing Self." *College Composition and Communication* 49.1 (February 1998): 45–62.

For Further Reading

Brooke, Robert, Ruth Mirtz, and Rick Evans. *Small Groups in Writing Workshops: Invitations to a Writer's Life.* Urbana, IL: NCTE, 1997.

Dillard, Jill, and Karin L. Dahl. "Collaborative Writing as an Option." *Teacher as Writer: Entering the Professional Conversation.* Ed. Karin L. Dahl. Urbana, IL: NCTE, 1992. 272–79.

Flores, Christopher. "Collaboration in Conflict: What Happens When Two Scholars Work Together on a Project—and Things Go Horribly Wrong?" *The Chronicle of Higher Education* 14 (June 2002): A14–16.

Gere, Anne Ruggles. *Writing Groups: History, Theory, and Implications.* Carbondale: Southern Illinois UP, 1987.

Howard, Rebecca Moore. "Plagiarisms, Authorships, and the Academic Death Penalty." *College English* 57.7 (November 1995): 788–806.

———. *Standing in the Shadow of Giants: Plagiarists, Authors, Collaborators.* Norwood: Ablex, 1999.

Hunter, Susan M. "The Case for Reviewing as Collaboration." *Rhetoric Review* 13.2 (1995): 265–69.

———. "Resurveying the Boundaries of Intellectual Property." *Foregrounding Ethical Awareness in Composition and English Studies.* Ed. Sheryl I. Fontaine and Susan M. Hunter. Portsmouth, NH: Heinemann Boynton/Cook, 1998. 160–73.

Hutcheon, Linda, and Michael Hutcheon. "A Convenience of Marriage: Collaboration and Interdisciplinarity." *PLMA* 116.5 (October 2001): 1364–75.

Lunsford, Andrea Abernethy. "Rhetoric, Feminism, and the Politics of Textual Ownership." *College English* 61.5 (May 1999): 529–44.

Lunsford, Andrea A., and Lisa Ede. "Collaborative Authorship and the Teaching of Writing." *The Construction of Authorship: Textual Appropriation in Law and Literature.* Ed. Martha Woodmansee, and Peter Jaszi. Durham, NC: Duke, UP, 1994. 417–38.

Lunsford, Andrea A., and Susan West. "Intellectual Property and
    Composition Studies." *College Composition and Communication* 47.3
    (October 1996): 383–411.

Trimbur, John. "Agency and the Death of the Author: A Partial Defense
    of Modernism." *JAC* 20.2 (2000): 283–98.

——. "Consensus and Difference in Collaborative Learning." *College
    English* 51 (October 1989): 602–16.

Woodmansee, Martha, and Peter Jaszi. "The Law of Texts: Copyright
    in the Academy." *College English* 57.7 (November 1995): 769–87.

York, Lorraine. *Rethinking Women's Collaborative Writing*. Toronto:
    U of Toronto P, 2002.

7

"So, Which Part Did You Write?": How Can I Manage the Politics of Collaborative Writing?

The ideologies of the academy take the autonomy of the individual—and of the author—for granted. [...] our examination of a number of university statements about PhD dissertations did not turn up a single explicit prohibition against collaborative dissertations. The most deeply held taboos are, after all, rarely specified in writing. [...] despite vigorous debates over theories and methods surrounding issues of subjectivity and authorship, ideologies of the individual and the author have remained largely unchallenged in scholarly practice.
—Lisa Ede and Andrea Lunsford (357, 358)

Every coauthored scholarly work defies academic custom, consciously or not, and perhaps the risks become fewer and fewer as more and more scholarly work boasts two or more names on the title page.
—Kami Day and Michele Eodice (158)

Why Do Writers Resist Collaborative Writing?

Take yourself back to the time before you began reading in this book about shifts in ideology about knowledge and the image of the writer. Recall, if you can, how you felt about collaborative writing. When you saw this book on the shelf in the bookstore required for the writing course you had signed up for, what was your reaction? Did you groan or sigh to yourself while remembering the collaborative teams you'd been "assigned" to in past courses and how one or two of you ended up doing most of the work while all the other team members earned the same credit for the project? Maybe you saw that this book was written by two people, and you wondered if the "first" author did more than the "second" author, if the first author was the leader or "creative spark" and the second author the follower or "plodding worker" (Ronald and Roskelly 259). If you are a creative writer who writes alone in the mythical "solitary garret," inspired by the Muse, you may have believed at the time you bought this book that for any piece of writing to be judged really good, it has to be the product of individual genius. And without being wholly conscious of what your reservations imply, you may have been ready to dismiss collaborative writing as lacking in quality and those who produce it as having gotten away with something, as having had to do only half the work.

If some of these judgments describe your initial reactions to the idea of collaborative writing, you are not alone. Indeed, the importance of individual achievement is a given in Western culture. Consider, for instance, the 2000 US Olympic swimmer who, having won many team gold medals, revealed in a TV interview the pressure she was under to win an individual gold medal for her accomplishment to really count. (She did not succeed in winning an individual gold medal that year.) Although you may expect to find examples of the devaluation of collaborative efforts in the world of sports, you needn't look much beyond the admissions office at the university to see similar assumptions at play in the educational system. In 2002, the admission committee at Duke University asked applicants to provide detailed explanations of how they composed their admissions essays. That is, they wanted to know who helped the writers and to what degree they used the feedback to fashion the final product; they wanted to find out if students' admission essays represented "their own work." (Brownstein A35, A37). If this attitude is representative of that of many *undergraduate* admission committees, then surely the applicant who hesitates to submit a team-authored proposal as a writing sample for admission to a *master*'s program is probably wise to hesitate. Unflattering judgments about collaborative writing come from students, too. During the course of drafting this very chapter, one of Susan's students stuck her head in the office doorway to ask what she was working on. Susan replied, "My latest book project." The student responded, "I hope you're writing this one by yourself this time."

In Western culture, the position of "All by myself," "All on my own" is automatically perceived as more highly valued than being part of a team or working with another person. This perception can be seen in play quite powerfully in the educational system where, despite Vygotsky's claim that "what children can do with the assistance of others might be in some sense even more indicative of their mental development than what they can do alone," standardized testing and academic grading policies presume the opposite: that only what students can do on their own demonstrates their mental abilities (qtd. in Roskelly 39).

Time for Reflection

Interview some of your peers or your students about their attitudes toward collaborative work. What has the experience of collaboration been like for them? How do they value a collaborative work compared to an individually authored text? Be sure to ask them where they think these values come from.

Facing the Facts in Academe

Given the negative attitudes toward collaboration that you've experienced and we've described in these scenarios, you may not be surprised to learn that Composition specialists who choose to write collaboratively meet with similar resistance and skepticism from faculty and administrative review committees. Here are a few snippets of some of their stories. When Lisa Ede came up for tenure in the mid-1980s, both she and her writing partner, Andrea Lunsford, were asked for "word counts for Ede's contributions to each of their coauthored publications," suggesting that the tenure committee suspected Ede was "incapable of first-rate scholarship" on her own (McNenny and Roen 8). Belanoff recalls that when she came up for promotion "one of the notes I got back when I handed in the file was that they wanted from the third edition of the textbook some idea of what I was responsible for. They wanted to know which parts were mine. Can I identify what in the textbook is mine?" (Interview).

Ronald and Roskelly have learned that their "knowledge is joined, shared, and communal—in inception, conception, and delivery." They "have given up the notion that anybody's idea is hers alone, although [...] much of the academy proceeds that way" (260). Having been asked the same question time and time again about the nature of her collaboration with Roskelly, Ronald notes that her "standard answer" to the question "How much of it is yours?" is "All of it." (Interview). Judith Entes explains in an essay that promotes coauthorship that she is the single author of the essay "in part because my supervisors—my department chair and my dean—strongly suggested that for professional advancement I should publish [...] *alone*" (47). When they were graduate students, Day and Eodice proposed a coauthored dissertation on collaboration in which they would write "collaboratively sentence by sentence, with the goal of building a dissertation that explored what happens when people write together" (1). Their Dean, however, claimed "that a jointly authored dissertation could not be considered unless the individual contributions of each student were clearly identified. In this particular case, that does not appear possible" (4).

Departmental guidelines for promotion and tenure reflect the skeptical views most English Studies faculty hold about collaborative scholarship. Goodburn and Leverenz cite what amounts to an explicit warning against collaborative scholarship in recent Florida State University English Department guidelines for promotion and tenure:

> While the Department recognizes the value of collaborative projects, we emphasize *the importance of establishing an independent reputation.* The Department has no guidelines about what proportion of your work should be independently authored, but you are undoubtedly in a better position if you have some clearly definable texts of your own in print (articles and book chapters) when you are considered for tenure. (qtd. in Goodburn and Leverenz 133, italics ours)

Another seemingly less negative example of how collaborative work might be considered in faculty review and evaluation is represented by the following directive in a Faculty Handbook:

> Candidates are responsible for noting instances where a teaching, scholarly, or professional service endeavor described in their narrative was a collaborative effort with another colleague or student. Further, they are responsible for ensuring the factual accuracy and appropriate acknowledgment of *their own level of contribution* for any collaborative teaching, scholarly, and/or professional service activities included in their narrative. (Review and Evaluation of Faculty Performance 5.40 for Kennesaw State University, italics ours)

Collaborative work will "count" in this system, but the implication is that faculty must be admonished not to pass off collaborative work as solely their own and to account for their "part," as "their own level of contribution." Evaluators have hierarchical expectations, wanting to know which hand held the pen where. Indeed, when collaborative writers are routinely asked to quantify and attribute their contributions, it reminds *all* writers that publications are treated as commodities in the economy of the academy. It is not uncommon to find faculty reviewers who believe that the first-author position on a publication means that that person did the most work and thus should be deemed the "principal" author.

This requirement at the administrative evaluation level to separate out and quantify the parts of a collaborative project denies two defining aspects of collaboration that we have put forth in previous chapters, one theoretical and one pragmatic: (1) that the nature of collaboration is something more than the sum of individual parts, and (2) that when two scholars engage in a collaborative project, the amount of work they undertake is not reduced but instead, doubles. And certainly we are not alone in our concern. This attention to quantity and the division of labor in the faculty evaluation process actually goes against the grain of the American Association of University Professors (AAUP), a nationally valued organization that serves to monitor and promote the work of professors. About collaboration, Committee B on Professional Ethics of the AAUP explains that,

> In [some] cases the collaboration is so intimate as to defy disentangling: the creativity is embedded in, and consequent upon, constant exchange of ideas and insights. This scholarly and psychological reality must be fully recognized in making academic decisions about the accomplishments and careers of single members of such combinations: what they have done must not be reduced to a second order of merit or worse, dismissed out of hand. (qtd. in McNenny and Roen 296)

Time for Reflection

Interview one of your favorite professors about his or her attitudes toward collaborative scholarship. Does he or she evaluate a work by an individual author differently from a work by two or more authors? What set of values does the professor bring to this evaluation process? If the professor has engaged in collaborative scholarship, ask him or her to share the story of how it was reviewed.

Working to Dispel Misconceptions

Day and Eodice, members of a new generation of collaborative writers, express in one of the epigraphs that opened this chapter their hope that the sheer incidence of collaborative scholarship will eventually make the practice seem less transgressive. Indeed, having read in Chapter 6 about the creative tensions that arise between writing partners, how they worked through and made decisions about voice-merging, ownership, and intellectual property, you, too, might have thought to yourself, "Well, that's that. Those issues are settled."

However, the experience of long-time collaborative writers Ede and Lunsford, who have been writing together and theorizing collaborative writing since 1984, can't be overlooked. Seventeen years since they first began writing about the misunderstandings surrounding collaborative writing, you can hear in the words of the first epigraph from a 2001 *PMLA* article that expanded on an MLA Presidential Forum address given in 2000, Ede and Lunsford's continuing concern and frustration. They believe that they must still argue for the value of collaborative writing and advocate that scholars in the humanities and in Composition write collaboratively because "ideologies of the individual and the author have remained largely unchallenged in scholarly practice" (358). As Ede and Lunsford's experiences and those of others you'll hear from in this chapter will demonstrate, you still need to understand how and why the larger world of academe may look askance at your decision to co-mingle as coauthors. By now, the foundational ideas we've been explaining in this book about how writing is inherently a social and collaborative process and how knowledge is constructed by means of an ongoing conversation may seem commonsensical to you—ideas so obvious as to be taken for granted. You'll find, however, that many of the colleagues you'll meet during your academic career will be unaware of these language theories, or, even if they are aware of them, they will not enact these beliefs in their scholarly writing or their professional evaluations. You may notice that they exhibit a disconnection between the postmodern theories of authorship they lecture on in the classroom and the values they enact in their professional practices.

We share the conviction of Amy Goodburn and Carrie Shively Leverenz, who learned to collaborate as graduate students and choose to collaborate as associate professors in English departments, "that the choice to collaborate within an institution that inhibits or devalues such collaboration must be made in full awareness of the risks as well as the potential benefits" (126). To that end, in this chapter we'll try to help you anticipate and deal with the arguments against and objections to collaborative scholarship that you may hear from mentors, peers, colleagues, administrators—and even your own students—in the future. We'll also discuss some underlying cultural reasons or sources for these objections so you'll understand where they're coming from.

Time for Reflection

In 2000, Andrea Lunsford and Lisa Ede set up a Web site—Collaborate!—to encourage collaborative writing and research in higher education at www.stanford.edu/group/collaborate. Visit the site to see what kind of information resides there and what kind of projects are represented there that would help you make a case for the value of collaborative scholarship.

Cultural Values That Resist Collaborative Scholarship

Remember how even some of the writing partners from whom you heard in Chapter 6, committed as they are to a social constructionist view of knowledge and writing, continue to feel the unresolved tension between individual autonomy and a shared voice. Yancey and Spooner describe this tension as "the tug and pleasure of working together in tension with the need to receive individual credit in a meritocracy." They claim that "[w]riters want collaboration and want separate identities, too" (50–51). Attempting to balance the desire to work together while remaining autonomous, Anson, Brady, and Larson decided to keep a dialogic journal to record their collaboration, but, at the same time, chose to keep "paper tracings of [their] collaboration as it evolves" so as not to lose track of their individual contributions (85). Another collaborative trio, Virginia Monseau, Jeanne Gerlach, and Lisa McClure, admits to the need to "retain [their] own individual voices" in the midst of their collaborative efforts to "make a book" (65). Not only, then, does the image of the writer writing alone and the notion of hierarchical collaboration remain ingrained in the minds of colleagues from English Studies and other academic disciplines, it can easily be a part of the thinking of those of us in Composition. The case those who choose to write collaboratively need to make is even more difficult given the fact that the tensions are likely to remain unresolved and the notions ingrained for those who collaborate as well as for those who evaluate the collaborations.

When we argued in Chapter 1 that to engage in dialogic collaborative writing, as we describe it throughout this book, you would need to be willing to change the way you think about knowledge and authorship, we were, in fact, asking you to adopt a mind set that calls into question prevailing cultural assumptions that cluster around a belief in the value of individual achievement. To elaborate these assumptions further for you and make clearer the change in thinking we are calling for, consider the work of four scholars from Composition and cognitive psychology. First, LeFevre, a noted Composition scholar, observes, "One would expect the predominant ideology of a society and its received views about the nature of human thought to affect and reinforce one another" (19). To illustrate this generalization, she focuses on the "enduring intellectual and cultural traditions that support a Platonic view" of writing as the private property of an individual mind: "traditions in literary studies emphasizing the individual unit as a focus of study; romantic notions of the isolated creator, inspired from within; and a strong regard for individualism in capitalistic, patriarchal societies" (22). Literary scholars who sit on review committees carry on the legacy of the New Critics removing the writer from time, place, and society. If they teach a composition course, these are the teachers who expect students to write by themselves and master citation practices not as evidence of their joining an ongoing conversation but to ensure against plagiarism. They also hold on to the Romantic image of the writer who writes alone, inspired from within. It is no wonder, then, that they subscribe to the belief that "individuals develop their own ideas from within and then claim ownership for what they invent [...] in line with the aims of Western capitalistic societies, in which ideas and discoveries [...] become property owned by individuals [...]" (LeFevre 22). These are the deep-seated, perhaps unacknowledged values that reviewers bring to the review of scholarship in the academy.

Second, in *Creative Collaboration,* cognitive psychologist Vera John-Steiner presents evidence culled from interviews and writings of collaborating partners in the humanities, the social sciences, the arts, and the sciences "to document how experienced thinkers engage in joint efforts as they struggle against society's pull toward individual achievement" (4). Her findings suggest how much the notions of developmental psychologist Jean Piaget continue to influence the way collaborative partnerships are judged. Piaget theorized in the late nineteenth century that intellectual development was totally in the control of the individual. Understandably, this emphasis from psychology reinforces the same sort of values that continue to hold sway in literary studies.

Finally, Composition scholars Day and Eodice interviewed ten teams of academics from across the humanities and social sciences and gathered information that corroborates much of what we've argued here about the material practices and affective dimensions of dialogic collaborative writing as they operate in contrast to "society's pull toward individual achievement" (John-Steiner 4). Day and Eodice's findings especially highlight the ways in which gender fits into the cluster of assumptions surrounding the image of the writer who writes alone. A masculinist view of writing emphasizes the product and the act of writing as a private activity of the self. The male-dominated academy values competition and hierarchy over collaboration and cooperation.

Arguments for the value of collaborative writing need to take into account these ideological positions. Collaborative writers need to accept that the readers of their work are likely to bring these preconceptions about individual authorship and coauthorship to the conference table whether they consciously realize it or not.

Are the Professional Risks of Coauthoring Worth It?

When choosing to write collaboratively, then, you must be ready to face the outside intrusions or external pressures that could quash your newfound enthusiasm for the generative power of collaborative writing. Institutions, departments, and even the discipline can foster an atmosphere in which creating knowledge with someone else by writing together is less valued than (seemingly) creating it by writing alone. Although you may be convinced by now that the solitary, originary author is a myth, you will have to acknowledge that for you and many academics vestiges of that belief system linger and complicate the decision to write collaboratively for pragmatic reasons related to career advancement. So does that mean that while you're coauthoring you should always also be single-authoring to establish your credentials? Does that mean you should postpone coauthoring until after you have tenure? After all, why should one coauthored book get two people two promotions? Doesn't that mean that one work is counting twice? Is a text better because it's coauthored? To answer these questions, you will have to make decisions about attribution and order of authorship that matter to your career advancement in school and beyond. The text on the page—the linear nature of printed text you and your coauthor have produced, rather than the process—has to be "explained" to review committees of all kinds.

So what can you do to convince external evaluators how valuable the cognitive and affective processes and the product of collaborative writing are, short of assigning them this book to read? It may always be a given that Composition specialists who choose to enact the epistemological understanding that makes them wary of competition, makes them question the possibility of truly individual achievement, will need to justify and explain their intellectual choices. To identify cognitive and affective dynamics of collaborative writing, your argument will be anecdotal and metacognitive. Reviewers may not be concerned with how collaboration à la Vygotsky enables an individual to mature in relation to others. It's the challenge you accept because you believe in the generative power and intrinsic value of collaborative writing.

Clearly, the obstacles to collaborative writing are not insurmountable. All the Composition specialists whose stories and advice you've read throughout this book have advanced in teaching and publishing careers. Many of them offer arguments you can use to explain and justify your choice to write collaboratively. According to Day and Eodice, for instance, collaborative scholarship has been justified in various disciplines

> by the complexity of large-scale research, by a variety of expertise, by the need to reduce isolation and sustain motivation, by improved productivity, elevated quality of products, the security to take risks, increased creativity and support, division of labor, increased potential for publication, generation of ideas, less procrastination, access to new research networks, and increased potential for theory building. (16)

Many writers who write with others share Ronald and Roskelly's observation that "there's a suspicion that writing together is somehow easier than writing alone; that somehow the writers escape work by halving their work load." In response to these questions about quantity and dialogic issues, Ronald and Roskelly argue that "the writing load doesn't split in half; it doubles" (260). Roskelly observes that "[...] it's far easier [...] to write as a single author than to do a collaboration. It takes longer to collaborate; it's more difficult to work through ideas. You've got two people who have found examples and stories [...] that need to be part of it so it's always a double process to filter that through" (Interview). Day and Eodice also encourage collaborative writers to resist dividing up the parts for the sake of suspicious evaluators, to talk instead about "intellectual contributions, what [was] learned from the project" and to "make visible the unique processes of [...] coauthorship, and articulate the value of [...] projects beyond the published product" (33). Other coauthors have asserted that the collective voice will represent their ideas better than the individual voice. For example, C. Mark Hurlbert and Michael Blitz say: "It was clear early on that the common goal was that we wanted to say things that mattered in the best possible way we could say them" (qtd. in Day and Eodice 83). And looking even more broadly, with a mind to transform the academy's value system, Roskelly suggests a commitment to "teaching courses where you talk about collaboration, encouraging the conditions for collaboration in the classroom, speaking back to people who question collaboration, asserting it [...] as a value" (Interview).

Keeping in mind the risks and advantages of coauthoring, the skeptisicm you'll receive, and responses we've described, we'd like to end this chapter with the encouraging perspective offered by Day and Eodice who feel certain that "the risks [will] become fewer and fewer as more and more scholarly work boasts two or more names on the title page" (158).

Trying Out Collaborative Writing

In pairs or teams of three or four, come up with a writing project that you agree to write collaboratively. Or select one that you have tried out in a previous chapter of this book. Imagine that a group of evaluators from areas of English Studies other than Composition—perhaps creative writers or British literature specialists—will be judging your collaborative scholarship. Brainstorm some arguments to use in a letter to justify the value of the collaborative work to such a committee of external evaluators. Then write the letter together.

Works Cited

Anson, Chris, Laura Brady, and Marion Larson. "Collaboration in Practice." *Writing on the Edge* 4.2 (Spring 1993): 80–96.

Belanoff, Pat. Telephone Interview. 1 May 2000.

Brownstein, Andrew. "Duke Asks Applicants If They Got Help on Essays, and Most Say They Did." *The Chronicle of Higher Education* 1 (March 2002): A35, A37.

Collaborate! www.stanford.edu/group/collaborate/.

Day, Kami, and Michele Eodice. *(First Person)²: A Study of Coauthoring in the Academy.* Logan: Utah State UP, 2001.

Ede, Lisa, and Andrea A. Lunsford. "Collaboration and Concepts of Authorship." *PMLA* 116.2 (2001): 354–69.

Elbow, Peter. *Embracing Contraries: Explorations in Learning and Teaching.* New York: Oxford UP, 1986.

Entes, Judith. "The Right to Write a Co-Authored Manuscript." Reagan, Fox, and Bleich 47–59.

Goodburn, Amy, and Carrie Shively Leverenz. " 'You Both Looked the Same to Me': Collaboration as Subversion." *The Dissertation and the Discipline: Reinventing Composition Studies.* Ed. Nancy Welch, Catherine G. Latterell, Cindy Moore, and Sheila Carter-Tod. Portsmouth, NH: Heinemann Boynton/Cook, 2002. 126–36.

John-Steiner, Vera. *Creative Collaboration.* New York and London: Oxford UP, 2000.

LeFevre, Karen Burke. *Invention as a Social Act.* Carbondale: Southern Illinois UP, 1987.

McNenny, Geraldine, and Duane H. Roen. "The Case for Collaborative Scholarship in Rhetoric." *Rhetoric Review* 10.2 (Spring 1992): 291–310.

——. "Collaboration or Plagiarism—Cheating is in the Eye of the Beholder." *Dialogue: A Journal for Writing Specialists* 1.1 (1993): 6–27.

Monseau, Virginia R., Jeanne M. Gerlach, and Lisa J. McClure. "The Making of a Book: A Collaboration of Writing, Responding, and Revising." Ed. Reagan, Fox, and Bleich. 61–75.

Reagan, Sally Barr, Thomas Fox, and David Bleich, eds. *Writing With: New Directions in Collaborative Teaching, Learning, and Research.* Albany: State U of New York P, 1994.

Ronald, Kate, and Hephzibah Roskelly. "Learning to Take it Personally." *Personal Effects: The Social Character of Scholarly Writing.* Ed. Deborah H. Holdstein, and David Bleich. Logan: Utah State UP, 2001. 253–66.

——. Personal Interview. 14 April 2000.

Roskelly, Hephizabah. *Breaking (into) the Circle: Group Work for Change in the English Classroom.* Portsmouth, NH: Heinemann Boynton/Cook, 2003.

Yancey, Kathleen Blake, and Michael Spooner. "A Single Good Mind: Collaboration, Cooperation, and the Writing Self." *College Composition and Communication* 49.1 (February 1998): 45–62.

For Further Reading

Ashton-Jones, Evelyn. "Coauthoring for Scholarly Publication: Should You Collaborate?" *Writing and Publishing for Academic Authors.* Ed. Joseph M. Moxley. Lanham, MD: UP of America, 1992. 269–87.

Creamer, Elizabeth G. and Associates. *Working Equal: Academic Couples as Collaborators.* New York: Routledge, 2001.

Ervin, Elizabeth, and Dana L. Fox. "Collaboration as Political Action." *Journal of Advanced Composition* 14.1 (1994): 53–71.

Gere, Anne Ruggles. *Writing Groups: History, Theory, and Implications.* Carbondale, IL: Southern Illinois UP, 1987.

Karell, Linda K. *Writing Together/Writing Apart: Collaboration in Western American Literature.* Lincoln: U of Nebraska P, 2002.

Leonardi, Susan J., and Rebecca A. Pope. "(Co)Labored Li(v)es; or, Love's Labors Queered." *PMLA* 116.3 (2001): 631–37.

——. "Screaming Divas: Collaboration as Feminist Practice." *Tulsa Studies in Women's Literature* 13 (1994): 259–70.

Lunsford, Andrea A., and Lisa Ede. "Rhetoric in a New Key: Women and Collaboration." *Rhetoric Review* 8.2 (Spring 1990): 234–41.

Miller, Susan. "New Discourse City: An Alternative Model for Collaboration." *Writing With: New Directions in Collaborative Teaching, Learning, and Research.* Ed. Sally Barr Reagan, Thomas Fox, and David Bleich. Albany: State U of New York P, 1994. 283–300.

Smith, John B. *Collective Intelligence in Computer-Based Collaboration.* Hillsdale, NJ: Lawrence Erlbaum Associates Publishers, 1994.

Stillinger, Jack. *Multiple Authorship and the Myth of Solitary Genius.* London and New York: Oxford UP, 1991.

Sullivan, Patricia A. "Revising the Myth of the Independent Scholar." *Writing With: New Directions in Collaborative Teaching, Learning, and Research.* Ed. Sally Barr Reagan, Thomas Fox, and David Bleich. Albany: State U of New York P, 1994. 11–29.

Welch, Nancy, Catherine G. Latterell, Cindy Moore, and Sheila Carter-Tod, eds. *The Dissertation and the Discipline: Reinventing Composition Studies.* Portsmouth, NH: Heinemann Boynton/Cook, 2002.

8

Writing Together While Being Apart: How Can Technology Support Co-Writing?

Their coauthoring style was a highly interactive one [...] On a word processor, Hunt or Vipond would draft a section and give the disk to the other, who would add, delete, or rewrite— marking changes with asterisks—and return the revised version to the other. This sequence was repeated time and time again over the months, with Vipond and Hunt taking turns initiating changes or additions. As drafts neared completion, the two met in final editing sessions in which they huddled over the same keyboard, reading (often aloud), discussing options, taking turns, adding and deleting, each occasionally even grabbing the keyboard out of the other's hands.

—Reither and Vipond (858)

They write together separately by email.
—Yancey and Spooner "A Single Good Mind" (45)

How Technology Has Worked for Us: Using Technology to Foster Collaboration

One of the questions we get asked about our collaborative writing partnership is "How do you manage to write together across time and space?" Needless to say, we don't have the luxury of sharing the keyboard or meeting in each other's offices down the hall on campus or brainstorming at a pajama party, as Belenky and her coauthors did, or sitting across the table from each other at McDonald's or the campus coffee shop as the "collaborwriters" Hal Blythe and Charlie Sweet did. Fifteen years ago when we started writing together, we lived only a few miles apart and had offices blocks away from one another; so it never occurred to us to imagine how we'd manage to write collaboratively if we were to become physically separated, as, indeed we have been for the past thirteen years by several time zones and thousands of miles of geography. And even if we had stopped to imagine how such distance could be accommodated in our writing process, we could never have imagined the technological changes that have so greatly affected our ability to continue writing together and the ways in which we accomplish this.

When Susan moved to Atlanta, we were in the midst of writing chapters and intertexts and assembling the manuscript for our first book, *Writing Ourselves into the Story.* In addition, we were revising a journal article that had just been accepted for publication, "Rendering the 'Text' of Composition." Although it may be difficult for some of you to conceive of such a situation, it was the case for us that just thirteen years ago, expensive long-distance phone calls and US mail were the basic technical means we used to finish these two projects. We had to ship $5\frac{1}{4}$-inch floppy disks and then $3\frac{1}{2}$-inch diskettes back and forth between Claremont and Atlanta in cardboard folders via US mail. Slow-moving modems didn't allow us easy access to e-mail or the Internet. Attachments in e-mail were unknown to us. We didn't yet have a Mouse to point and click at the icons in the graphical interface that Microsoft Windows provides. Saving a document "as" rich text format (RTF) was unheard of. We were still using WordPerfect for DOS with its Shift F-plus-a-number function keys on our PCs. And we didn't always own compatible versions of the software. We didn't yet have cell phones with unlimited long distance contracts or high-speed Internet access or Internet service providers for our home computers. We didn't even have the mobility provided by laptops.

The constraints of time and distance have certainly been mitigated over the years by the technologies now available to us. In the extended process of writing this book together, we gained access to a wide range of facilitative technologies: the conversational potential of e-mail and instant messaging, the speed of the Internet, the editing and tracking features of Microsoft Word, the ease of attaching documents as Word files or RTF files in e-mail, the seemingly free cell phone minutes, laptops,

24/7 Internet access to our e-mail at school, access to NetLibrary and all sorts of electronic databases for research. These technologies became progressively available to the world and to us as we moved through our collaborative projects. And as each became available, we learned how to use them, how to determine their benefits to us, and then selected those most useful for our collaborative writing process.

What Our Process Looks Like

We want to emphasize here that technology fosters collaboration, but it doesn't ensure or in any way make collaboration happen. Indeed, the technologies we describe in this chapter came into existence long after our collaborative writing began. Thousands of writers have written together—even though they lived in different parts of a town or country—without the use of computers, fax machines, or even telephones. Technology is not a starting place for collaboration, rather it is a tool that makes collaboration easier. Our collaboration was long established before we developed the uses of technology that would become our *modus operandi* for writing together.

For us, early in the process, we use our computers individually to sketch out quickly our projects and freewrite segments of text. These documents are easily converted to compatible rich text files and embedded in or attached to electronic messages sent nearly instantaneously from one time zone to another where they can just as easily be placed back into the other's document file for cutting and pasting, adding and deleting. Each time the growing, changing document makes its way from Georgia to California and back, the singularity of our voices becomes less visible. Initially, we carefully date each draft we send and use Microsoft Word's "tracking" tool as a way to "see" what the other has added or deleted or changed. A barrage of e-mail messages occur in the midst of these file exchanges as we raise possibilities to one another, let the other know what we are attempting to do, ask for reaction or ideas. But after two or three exchanges, the e-mail slows, and the various colors to indicate layers of changes in the text become distracting. So we "turn off" the tracking, accept the changes and, both metaphorically and literally, seem to have arrived at our third voice.

Technology has allowed us to enter into one other's writing in a way that couldn't occur if we were retyping manuscripts. The sending back and forth of text and several rounds of writing into the text we receive make it much easier for us to lose ourselves and create a new writer, a third voice. In addition, you'll notice that we arrive at our third voice by using the technology as a facsimile for conversation/talk that we would have were we able to write together, face to face, side by side. While we have rarely composed together at a computer screen, sharing the point of utterance, as some writing teams do, conversation has always been a critical component of our collaborative process. The technology we use—e-mails, exchanged files, embedded comments and tracked changes—emulates the free-form, back-and-forth nature of conversation/talk.

Problem Solving and Learning New Technologies

Of course, all writers, not just those of us who choose to write collaboratively, need to be mindful of what Cynthia and Richard Selfe have named the "politics of the interface." Computer interfaces like all communication acts and tools are never value-free, are always interested, and writers need to be "technology critics as well as technology users" (C. Selfe and R. Selfe 496). The writing and communication environments that we have been using over the years to collaborate with their various visual, textual, and interactive rhetorical strategies embedded in the designs of the graphical interfaces for e-mail, word processing, file transfer, and Internet access no doubt have *determined* the nature of the process we have engaged in. Certainly, the "default subject" for any of the technology we use is *not* a pair of writers who are engaged in the kind of dialogic collaboration we've been describing throughout this book. As much as the technology has facilitated our work together, we have had to adapt our ways to the computer interfaces available to us.

Moving from this ideological concern to a more nuts-and-bolts level, as much as it has facilitated our writing, the use of technology to work on our collaborative projects has created its own set of obstacles, road-blocks, and frustrations. For example, at the same time that e-mail emulates conversation, it also has its own distinctive rhetorical qualities. An e-mail message written hastily between classes along with the absence of facial expressions and the human voice has, from time to time, led to misunderstandings or misreadings. Certainly such misunderstandings have not been so problematic as to endanger a project or a friendship, but we both have become sensitive to the possibility of their occurrence and know the value of a parenthetical explanatory comment or a follow-up phone conversation. Aside from this kind of rhetorical difficulty, there are the countless technological ones: using conflicting platforms and programs that prevent us from "reading" files, working at home on slower or less capable computers than those at school, accommodating changes in software that our schools make, being unable to unzip files, and differences that occur due to our having different Internet providers at school and at home. Each time one of these problems occurs, we lose some time and, inevitably, experience a degree of frustration. But we always manage to see our way through and have come to realize that as long as technology continues to change, an integral part of the process of our collaborative writing will include being ready to solve the problems we encounter.

Ironically, the same technology that fosters our collaboration also makes us more and more impatient. Waiting 3–5 days for a disk in the mail was somehow much less difficult than waiting 3–5 seconds for a file to download. As the technology advances, our expectations rise and, at the same time, we are unable to "keep up" with all that is new. There are undoubtedly new or alternate technologies that we don't have time to investigate and learn. In the middle of a collaborative project, we don't want to stop to learn a new program and lose the rhythm of our writing. We are left to find time between projects to learn something new. To a certain extent, then, the technologies we have chosen to use reflect our own level of skill and of access to various technologies. What is comfortable and effective for one set of writers may not be for another. For example, some of you may be especially comfortable with and adept at using various forms of synchronous communication—chat rooms, instant messaging, or multimedia conferencing. But for the moment, we still experience widely uneven access to the hardware and software necessary for such communication. Phone calls continue to be the best form of synchronous communication to support our particular reliance on talk to conceive and advance our collaborative projects.

Time for Reflection

How did you learn to work in electronic writing environments? Has the technology been transparent for you, or have you had to struggle with it to make it work for your individual composing process? How do you think that the technology you have used has influenced or changed the way you go about working on a writing project?

How Technology Has Worked for Other Collaborative Writers

Our experiences as coauthors are by no means unique. Many of those with whom we have spoken or whose accounts we've read have had to face the difficulties of writing together while living apart. And at some point, each pair or group has gratefully embraced technology to help them write collaboratively. Writers who have had the opportunity to write both without and with the technology easily see its benefits and would agree with Lunsford and Ede who acknowledge that the pragmatic constraints of being physically separated are greatly reduced by today's technology (126–27). Peter Mortensen recalls that "actually [not having] the technology was a real big deal. I can remember when (a coauthor) and I [...] [were] express mailing diskettes back and forth between Detroit and Lexington, and there was a delay, and it was expensive, and there was just a lot of expense [...] to have updated drafts to one another" (E-mail). Similarly, Knoblauch and Brannon recall writing without technology: "When we first started writing together, we decided whose name would go first by who typed the final draft. After our first book we bought our first computer together. The drudgery of typing did not work then for placing our names on articles [...] new technologies have made our problems in that period largely obsolete" (E-mail).

Practically speaking, we have found that coauthors use technology in the course of generating ideas, managing the plans for a project, integrating sections, reviewing and editing text, and making decisions or resolving disagreements. Moreover, writers tend to immerse their co-writing process in technology like Ronald and Roskelly who explain that "When we are writing together long distance [...] we talk, write, email, fax, read over the phone, revise separately, revise together" (261). Descriptions like this one highlight the way in which computers, phones, and fax machines have become significant—almost inextricable or invisible—components of the collaborative writing process, making long-distance collaboration a possibility and creating for its co-writers a "proximity" nearly equal to that of the writers who have the luxury of sitting side by side.

If we tease out the most frequently mentioned use of technology—other than the telephone—it would be the fast-paced exchange allowed through e-mail. Hans Ostrom, speaking of his collaboration with Wendy Bishop, describes the way in which e-mail narratives became a way to learn the other's style and voice. He explains that, "[Wendy] and I talk endlessly in person and on e-mail and know each other's writing style best in dialogue and story." Agreeing with her coauthor, Wendy added that "we started with letters and moved to e-mail and e-mail lets us 'phone home' at anytime. Sometimes it's a pick-me-up— what would you do? Sometimes it's a negotiation: okay, what are we going to write next? And sometimes it's commiserating. But mostly about writing (which for us includes talk of family, moods, departments, genre, weather and the world). Without e-mail, I expect we'd send drafts by snail mail again or twenty-mule teams through death valley" (E-mail).

Kathleen Yancey and Michael Spooner use e-mail in order to "write together separately" ("A Single Good Mind" 45). Certainly their explanation captures the value of e-mail and the depth and breadth of its effect on authors. They claim that e-mail "feels like a hybrid form, combining elements one would expect in letters, on the phone, or in face-to-face conversation" ("Postings" 254).

And once the writers have generated a text between them, technology becomes a significant tool for revision. Elbow expresses great affection for how this tool can promote a true, collaborative revision: "[. . .] what I really find most precious is this crudely simple method where one person starts it and the other person takes the disk and just does it, makes the revision, and the start is very primitive so the revision is very major. But then when it goes back to the first person, that person might make nontrivial changes [. . .]. And there, too, we didn't talk about it. We just maltreated each other's text" (Interview).

Still, some writers have identified complications in the very technologically aided processes that others have praised. The most sensitive issue is that of the writer's voice and individual identity. While we are not alone in celebrating the emergence of the third voice that is not that of any one writer, other writers find the idea of such a merged voice troubling, even to the point of wanting to avoid it altogether. For example, speaking of the same "maltreatment" of text that Elbow finds exciting, Anson and his co-writers approached the merging of voices with great caution and much discussion. These writers "discovered that as our collaboration progressed, it became increasingly difficult to see who wrote what because the combination of reading, writing, and conversing—especially on the fluid medium of the word processor—erased discourse boundaries, erased ownership, and foregrounded the practical negotiations involved in creating a collective text" (87). Ultimately, they had to develop a writing strategy that would accommodate their uneasiness about losing identities and their need to write a collaborative text:

this single, "dialogic" notebook—composed on computer disk and exchanged among the three of us (a hybrid compromise between e-mail and regular correspondence)—allowed us to identify other textual goals by conversing about diverse aspects of collaboration. The notebook also gave us a trace of our collective pre-writing and has helped us to reconstruct issues and ideas as they came up naturally in our own thinking [...] Since we all entered the dialogic notebook and wrote into (sometimes over) each other's entries, we can no longer tell where one person's words end and another's begin (Anson, Brady, and Larson 83–84)

Taking this concern even further and believing strongly in the importance of not letting voices merge, Belenky claims that "If you send your disk around and people start changing it, your words and theirs get merged too fast; you need some sort of a balance. Writing collaboratively gets very confusing because, when you're really working together, when the dialogue really starts, ideas grow and change and no one has real ownership. Yet you have to keep, or you ought to keep, your own voice" (Ashton-Jones and Thomas 32). Echoing these same thoughts more succinctly, Spooner and Yancey insist that there is no "blender-voice" for them—there is room for "two separate soapboxes at the end" ("Postings on a Genre of E-mail" 253). Elsewhere, too, they choose to retain the e-mail format of their dialogues to resist merging voices, "to retain and express the multivocal conversation [they] experienced" ("Concluding the Text" 313).

Time for Reflection

How do you feel about the idea of how the use of technology can so easily produce a "third voice?" Do you believe it's possible or even advisable for co-writers to lose their individual voices? What experiences with technology in particular led you to your conclusions?

Specialized Technologies Marketed for Collaboration

Looking at publishers' catalogues, searching the Internet, or reading advertisements in magazines and journals, one can quickly find numerous software programs marketed for what their designers call "collaboration." But this label can be misleading. It is necessary to distinguish between the kind of collaborative writing we've been describing and advocating throughout this book and collaboration in instructional settings. These software programs most often provide ways to enable and support collaborative pedagogies. So although these programs are billed as being tools of collaboration, the collaboration they refer to is not a dialogic form among consenting writers, but, rather, a hierarchical form that exists in the classroom when students are "assigned" the task of collaboration or a limited form that occurs after the author has composed in a solo setting and a "reviewer" is invited to respond and "collaborate" with the draft. These severely limited forms of so-called collaboration are easy to identify in the advertisements of some prominent programs:

> CommonSpace provides an almost unlimited electronic workspace in which to write, comment, and revise. By opening and closing multiple workspaces containing various drafts and linked commentary, students can see all iterations of a paper at the same time in a single document—capturing a complete history of the project.

Microsoft Office XP lets you "work smarter with others" and "Compare and Combine changes easily with Send for Review. Manage multiple comments and revisions from within a single document."

Adobe Acrobat 5.0 lets writers review and comment digitally (markup.pdf). Indeed advertisers claim that

> Now it's easier to gather everyone's feedback—valuable or not—all in one convenient digital file. With the full version of Adobe Acrobat 5.0 software you can add comments to any document. Review and approval is faster and easier when you convert your document to a universal adobe PDF. Users can comment digitally using highlights, strike-throughs, approval stamps and even electronic sticky notes. So you can share feedback with colleagues and speed up the turnaround and approval process dramatically. No multiple hard copies. No delays. No hassle. Now everyone can make all the comments they want. Even if you choose to ignore them.

Similarly, although an ad for *Daedalus Online*, which was "developed by top composition scholars," promises the potential writing-instructor-users the capability to "Explore the newest innovation in collaborative writing" and "facilitate a shared writing process among students," the promise of collaboration peters out with the following: "Students [. . .] can now [. . .] employ prewriting strategies, partake in computer-mediated real-time conferencing, and post feedback to discussion board."

Although any one of these programs we've cited—and there are many more we didn't include—could be adapted for use by those of us who are actually writing together, we are not the target audience the designers of these programs have in mind.

How Technology May Support Collaborative Writers in the Future

There is no doubt that technology has become an integral part of all writing and, in its own way, of collaborative writing. As we suggested at the beginning of this chapter, it is difficult to predict just where technological advances will go from here and how they will impact collaborative writing in the future. Certainly, one obvious area of interest and development is in providing ever-more effective electronic means for supporting activities that normally take place in face-to-face meetings. We, therefore, anticipate developments in synchronous capabilities of communication as it becomes easier for co-writers to see and hear one another as they sit thousands of miles away. And as technology more realistically emulates "[t]hese characteristics of face-to-face exchanges [. . .] group members [may be able to] to experiment more freely with exploring differences in individual approaches to problems, writing tasks, and issues" (Selfe 147).

The future intersection of technology and collaborative writing may also lead writers and researchers to reconsider the idea of authoring itself. Perhaps some of the most long-standing concepts about the solo nature of writing and the ownership of language, concepts that we have tried to shake loose in this book, have emerged as much from the technologies of writing as they did from the actual nature of composing. Consider Peter Holland's claim that "with hypertext there is no way to differentiate 'original' texts from revisions or additions made by subsequent readers/writers. Electronic writing environments are thus changing our understanding of the concept of 'author,' creating 'two types of author/editors, refusing to distinguish between the two: those who write sentences and those who restructure materials'" (qtd. in Spigelman 8). Perhaps there will no longer be a need to "teach" collaboration as the concept and processes become inextricable from the way writing is produced.

Trying Out Collaborative Writing

In Chapter 1, you passed around a sheet of paper to your classmates in order to create a piece of collaborative writing. Try a similar activity using a computer diskette or CD-rom. That is, working in groups of 3 or 4, have the first member of the group write a page-long "text" about the importance and risks of creating a collaboratively "merged-voice." Each group member will then take a turn writing "into" the text, using, if possible, a tracking device to record the changes he or she makes. When each person has had an opportunity to write, read the "final" version and then each of you write (in your notebook) some reactions/reflections about this composing process.

Works Cited

Adobe Acrobat 5.0. The Chronicle of Higher Education (3 May 2002): A7.

Anson, Chris, Laura Brady, and Marion Larson. "Collaboration in Practice." *Writing on the Edge* 4.2 (Spring 1993): 80–96.

Ashton-Jones, Evelyn, and Dene Kay Thomas. "Composition, Collaboration, and Women's Ways of Knowing: A Conversation with Mary Belenky." *(Interviews): Cross-Disciplinary Perspectives on Rhetoric and Literacy.* Ed. Gary A. Olson, and Irene Gale. Carbondale: Southern Illinois UP, 1991. 27–44.

Bishop, Wendy, and Hans Ostrom. E-mail. 27 September 2000.

CommonSpace. Boston: Sixth Floor Media, n.d.

Daedalus Online. Boston: Addison Wesley Longman, n.d.

Elbow, Peter, and Pat Belanoff. Telephone Interview. 1 May 2000.

Fontaine, Sheryl I., and Susan Hunter. "Rendering the 'Text' of Composition." *Journal of Advanced Composition* 12.1 (Fall 1992): 395–406.

——. *Writing Ourselves Into the Story: Unheard Voices from Composition Studies.* Carbondale: Southern Illinois UP, 1993.

Knoblauch, Cy, and Lil Brannon. E-mail. 20 February 2001

Lunsford, Andrea A., and Lisa Ede. "Collaboration and Compromise: The Fine Art of Writing with a Friend." *Writers on Writing.* Volume II. Ed. Tom Waldrep. New York: Random House, 1988. 121–27.

Microsoft Office XP. WA: Microsoft Corporation, 2001.

Mortensen, Peter. Personal Interview. 15 April 2000.

Reither, James, and Douglas Vipond. "Writing as Collaboration."
    College English 51.8 (1989): 855–67.
Ronald, Kate, and Hephzibah Roskelly. "Learning to Take it
    Personally." *Personal Effects: The Social Character of Scholarly
    Writing*. Ed, Deborah H. Holdstein, and David Bleich. Logan:
    Utah State UP, 2001. 253–66.
Selfe, Cynthia L. "Computer-Based Conversations and the Changing
    Nature of Collaboration." *New Visions of Collaborative Writing*.
    Ed. Janis Forman. Portsmouth, NH: Boynton/Cook, 1992. 147–69.
Selfe, Cynthia L., and Richard J. Selfe, Jr. "The Politics of the Interface:
    Power and Its Exercise in Electronic Contact Zones." *College
    Composition and Communication* 45.4 (December 1994): 480–504.
Spigelman, Candace. *Across Property Lines: Textual Ownership in Writing
    Groups*. Carbondale: Southern Illinois UP, 2000.
Yancey, Kathleen, and Michael Spooner. "Concluding the Text: Notes
    toward a Theory and the Practice of Voice." *Voices on Voice:
    Perspectives, Definitions, Inquiry*. Ed. Kathleen Blake Yancey.
    Urbana, IL: NCTE, 1994. 298–314.
——. "Postings on a Genre of E-mail." *College Composition and
    Communication* 47.2 (May 1996): 252–78.
——. "A Single Good Mind: Collaboration, Cooperation, and the
    Writing Self." *College Composition and Communication* 49.1
    (February 1998): 45–63.

For Further Reading

Condon, Frances V. "The Ethics of Teaching Composition in
    Cyberspace: Knowledge Making in Commodified Space."
    Foregrounding Ethical Awareness in Composition and English Studies.
    Ed. Sheryl I. Fontaine, and Susan M. Hunter. Portsmouth,
    NH: Boynton/Cook Heinemann, 1998. 37–51.
Selfe, Cynthia L. "Technology and Literacy: A Story about the Perils of
    Not Paying Attention." *College Composition and Communication*
    50. 3 (February 1999): 411–36.
Sharples, Mike, ed. *Computer Supported Collaborative Writing*. London:
    Springer-Verlag, 1993.

9

A Collaborative Essay on Collaborative Writing: What More Can We Learn from Writers Who Write Together?

How Did This Project on Collaborative Writing Begin?

As we've already indicated, the beginnings of this book project can be traced to coffee shops and college offices in Claremont, California, fifteen years ago, when we first met and shared ideas and professional concerns and began the slow, careful process of committing to a long friendship and collaboration. It has been through our various experiences with writing together—through the years of figuring out how to write together, as personal and professional circumstances change—that we have come to share a deep appreciation for the process of writing together. This appreciation was apparent in our scholarship, where we wrote about the nature of editorial response, and it was apparent in our early "demonstrations" of collaboration. Like other pairs of collaborative writers—Lisa Ede and Andrea Lunsford, Kate Ronald and Hephzibah Roskelly, Michael Spooner and Kathleen Yancey—we wanted to show others what collaboration looked like. And so we presented conference papers by reading in alternating voices; we wrote essays in the form of collages that literally "pieced together" the voices of many others; and we structured roundtable discussions at professional meetings that openly invited audience participation.

But even after all of these collaborative demonstrations, something was still missing. It is very difficult to make the collaboratively produced products published in journals and delivered at conferences "look" any different from those that have been produced by a single author. In the demonstrations that we and others have performed, we try to make these differences visible—read aloud together, read in alternating voices, invite members of the audience to read, speak as if in conversation—but in the end, these are demonstrations, play-acting; they are not collaborative writing. And they don't really make visible the intertwining of minds, the shuffling thoughts of two or more individuals, the emergence of harmony that occurs in collaborative writing.

Ultimately, we were not satisfied merely with writing about the value of writing together or with creating demonstrative moments of collaboration for others to view. Being proponents of the process wasn't enough—and what was missing was the very process itself. If we believed in the value of writing together, then we needed to step from behind the conference podium or the pages of the journal, to stop telling others *about* the process and, instead, *engage* them in its *doing*. We noticed others had made this same journey, from writing about collaboration to demonstrating the process to engaging others in it, like Andrea Lunsford and Lisa Ede whose Web site enjoins others in the humanities to "Collaborate!" We, too, had to become activists.

For us, the most accessible place to engage in such activism was the classroom, where we were both already having our own students write together. If we could reach students—novices in our discipline—then we would be planting seeds that would have time to germinate and grow and, potentially, fertilize others. But how could we get into others' classrooms and reach their students, too? The obvious answer: Write a textbook. Our project, then, became to write this text, one that not only talks about writing together and lauds its benefits, but encourages you, the students, to write together and, in fact, provides opportunities and ways to make this happen. Because we believe there is no one "best way" to collaborate or one "definitive story" of collaboration, the text we envisioned—the one we have, in fact, written—would have to include the voices of others in our discipline who write together.

That is why in previous chapters we've used some of our own experiences and the stories of five other pairs of practicing collaborative writers, to describe what we've come to know as the value and idiosyncrasies of collaborative writing. We wanted you to understand the hows and whys of this complex, theoretically important, politically charged professional activity. And we now want to invite you to join the community of Composition specialists who choose to write collaboratively. We invite you to listen to the voices of others who have written together and then to accept our invitation for you to collaborate.

But Isn't Collaborative Writing an Old Story?

What those of you new to Composition Studies may not know is that for some time now, Composition specialists have agreed that collaborative writing is a respected process that achieves valuable results for both writers and readers. Since its publication in 1990, *Singular Texts/Plural Authors* by Ede and Lunsford has become the generative text for countless journal articles and edited collections on the subject. These scholarly discussions of the values of collaborative writing rely on data from research in the workplace and from anecdotal accounts to build their arguments about the distinctive characteristics of the collaborative process and collaborative writing, its importance to the profession, and the need for students at all levels to be prepared to write with others. However, in spite of these numerous and well-argued publications, collaborative writing still occurs less frequently than single-authored writing and appears less frequently in scholarly journals and books in Composition than single-authored writing. The low occurrence, we believe, is *not* because editors in Composition Studies are unwilling to publish coauthored articles. As recently as the December, 2000 Modern Language Association Presidential Forum, Ede and Lunsford admit that single authorship thrives and that institutional barriers to writing together and reward structures that privilege single-authored work over coauthored work continue to dominate academia ("Collaboration and Concepts of Authorship"). Day and Eodice more recently in (*First Person*)[2]: *A Study of Coauthoring in the Academy* have conducted qualitative interviews with academics to describe the benefits of collaborative authorship. What we are pointing to here is an apparent contradiction in the discipline. For although we and others like us in Composition have been tenured and promoted at a variety of institutions of higher education on the basis of—and in spite of—our coauthored scholarship, collaborative writing teams are still more the exception than the rule. Though it has been authorized and certified by the discipline, collaborative writing remains relatively uncommon in our professional lives and literature and unfamiliar to students in Composition Studies courses.

So What Would Have to be Done to Change This?

While there are numerous institutional and political reasons to explain why collaborative writing continues to hold a peripheral position in our field, there is also a significant pedagogical reason that emerges from our classrooms. Although many of us have written about collaboration for one another in professional journals and books, we have done little to introduce students entering into Composition research and pedagogy to either the theoretical underpinnings of collaborative writing or the practical concerns of the process and its implications. Unless we provide explanations and instructions about collaborative writing that are written for and directed to students—you who are novices in the field who will become practicing members of Composition—it is unlikely that the intellectual value we have bestowed upon collaborative writing will become rooted in the professional behavior of our discipline. Those of us who write collaboratively need to provide sustained discussion and instruction for our students on this subject. Indeed, if we in Composition truly believe that knowledge is socially constructed, that "all writing is collaboration," that "writing is a social act," then we need to be encouraging students like you to try on the fluid roles of collaborative writing, to participate within its loosely structured confines and to consider the value of "the creative tension inherent in [. . .] [the] multivoiced and multivalent ventures" of collaborative writing—to engage in what Ede and Lunsford have called the "dialogic mode" of collaborative writing (*Singular Texts/Plural Authors* 133).

In order to appreciate collaborative writing as a distinct creative behavior, a way of thinking, and a mode of inquiry for the discipline, we have written this book as an effort to help students untangle the complexities of the process of writing together: to examine the personal and professional exigencies for collaborative writing, the qualities that make collaborative writing something more than just an efficient way to get work done; to explore how reading and teaching change in light of collaborative writing, how our institutions and graduate programs allow for, value, or encourage collaborative writing, and, moreover, how the template of solitary authorship may be so etched in one's own writing traditions that collaboratively authored work is unconsciously devalued.

But Don't Most Students Already *Do* Collaborative Writing in Their Classes?

As some of you reading this book know, many instructors do already ask their students to engage in some kind of collaborative writing task and present to them the value of this kind of writing: It is most like the writing they will do in the workplace; it makes a large project more manageable; it creates a comfortable community in an anonymous university environment. While these arguments certainly are valid, they don't come close to capturing the most essential value of collaborative writing that we have presented throughout this text. The larger, more encompassing argument for the value of collaborative writing is that once a writer truly understands collaborative writing, he or she will also understand something about the writing process that she didn't before. Indeed, we have gone so far as to say that *unless* a writer understands collaborative writing as a dialogic, meaning-making process, she cannot really understand writing. We believe that collaborative writing mirrors the social act of *all* writing and that engaging in it allows writers to experience the social aspect of writing explicitly and incontrovertibly.

At the Conference on College Composition and Communication in 2000, Ronald and Roskelly in their presentation on "Women Taking Students Seriously" asked why questions remain about making students the center of educational agendas. They asked, "What kind of action still needs to be taken to transform the composition classrooms we know into the ones we've been imagining?" In their talk, they gave us a way to think about what was still missing from our own and others' advocacy for collaborative writing when they reminded us of what Paulo Freire calls in *The Pedagogy of the Oppressed* (89–90) a "limit situation." We extrapolated from their position about taking action to break down barriers to student-centered learning an explanation for our own deeply held belief in the value of collaborative writing and what we wanted to do to enact that belief. For us, the continued dominance of solo authoring in our classrooms and scholarship presents itself as what Freire would call a "barrier," "obstacle," or "limit" that prevents writers from participating in the creative, knowledge-making properties of dialogic collaborative writing.

We trust that having read the first eight chapters, you can understand the activity of collaborative writing as being more than just an "efficient" way to write or a reflection of workplace practice. Rather, collaborative writing is a "limit-act," "directed at negating and overcoming, rather than passively accepting the 'given'," in this case, solo writing. And so, we advocate collaborative writing as a "transforming response" that purposefully takes the constructionist nature of all writing—even solo—and builds and relies on it.

Those of us who have written with others know quite well that there are tremendous differences between the process of writing alone and writing together, specifically in how, when, where, and why these processes happen and how others receive and judge the products. Collaborative writing is compatible with the profile of language as a conversation, a dialogue, a tool for solving problems, a means of making knowledge. Indeed, as we've pointed out repeatedly in previous chapters, the more common image of the writing process—that of a solo writer—belies the social, instrumental, collaborative nature of language. The writer who writes with others is engaged in the recursive, two-way, turn-taking process of sustained, ongoing conversation and dialogue. And like any synergistic activity, the combined effect of the interaction of two or more writers is greater than the sum of their individual effects. To think otherwise makes collaborative writing an aberrant activity tacked on to a curriculum or turned to when writers are lonely or "blocked" rather than a writing process that grows out of the very nature of language.

You Keep Saying "We Believe." What About the Experiences of Other Collaborative Writers?

As our own collaboration came to focus on the topic of collaborative writing and guiding students toward their own experiences with collaborative writing, we knew that, among other things, we wanted to learn more from others who write together. Some stories are already available, but, as is our way, we wanted to hear the unheard stories from familiar pairs of writers who were thinking about writing together in the same way we were, but who hadn't yet spoken about it. Our goal was to add to the lore about writing together, to make a more detailed representation of "collaborwriting." And so, using our own experience of writing together along with Belenky's account of the genesis and composition of *Women's Ways of Knowing* and Blythe and Sweet's essay entitled "Collaborwriting," we formulated a list of questions to ask other writers about the material, logistical, and epistemic conditions that drew them together. Indeed, from these questions and answers grew the chapters of this book:

1. What circumstances led to your decision to write together?
2. What is the role of conversation or talk when you are working on a project?
3. How does writing collaboratively help you sustain response and revision, prolong your composing process, resist closure?
4. What changes did you have to make in the way you write to move from solo to collaborative writing?
5. How has your experience with collaborative writing changed the way you write "alone?"
6. How do you manage the politics and creative tensions of collaborative writing?
7. How do you handle questions of ownership of language and ideas when you write together?
8. How do you manage to continue to write together when you are separated by time and distance?

We never set out, however, to be systematic researchers seeking data that we could code or label in some formal way; we simply wanted to gather stories of collaborative writers in order to confirm and even extend our own premises about collaborative writing. And so, our collection of stories is varied and informal: Due to circumstances of time and distance, some of them responded in person, some by phone conversation, and others by e-mail exchange. These different media affected the responses in different ways: Some person-to-person settings were more conducive to talk than others; some taped interviews were more accurately transcribable than others; some writing pairs are more loquacious than others. Differences aside, the pairs of writers let us eavesdrop on written and spoken reflections about their own experiences writing together.

Throughout the course of reading this book, you have heard from Wendy Bishop and Hans Ostrom, Peter Mortensen and Janet Carey Eldred, Pat Belanoff and Peter Elbow, Kate Ronald and Hephzibah Roskelly, and Lil Brannon and Cy Knoblauch, all of whom generously agreed to answer our questions and consented to our using their responses in this book. For this final chapter, we have selected responses from each interview and used these to "render" the writers' voices and to create for you some more extensive portraits of collaborative writing as it emerges from these pairs of writers. Rather than providing these portraits in the shape of a formal essay with transitions, analyses, comparisons, and summaries, we will simply present the writers' own words and ask you to collaborate with what you read to find ways in which the pairs are different from and similar to one another. In the fragments of conversations you're about to read, we expect you will hear emerging issues of trust and confidence, ownership and property, personal connection, and professional worth. What you read or hear in these exchanges between writing partners will reiterate and reprise some of what you've already read in this book; it may also raise new ideas or new concerns about collaborative writing.

Using the questions we provide in each "Time for Reflection," we invite you to engage in collaborative analysis of the interviews asking, "What did you hear? What fits with your experiences and assumptions? What features of collaboration are emerging? What do you think you can learn from the stories of writers who work together?"

What Did They Say?

Peter Elbow and Pat Belanoff

During a tape-recorded phone call in May 2000, Peter Elbow and Pat Belanoff shared these reflections with us about writing together. They responded to the questions we posed in terms of their textbook, *A Community of Writers,* which they were in the process of revising, in terms of essays on portfolios, and in terms of their years working together to develop the writing program at SUNY Stony Brook.

PAT.   [...] since [Peter] hired me [at Stony Brook], he'd obviously already made the decision that we could at least work together in probably some way, shape, or form. [...] But I think for me at least, my relationship with Peter has always had that personal side to it [...] somehow we got along personally as well, and I don't know about how that works [...] with collaboration and whether there's people collaborating for whom that's not true.

PETER.   So we're writing together because we happened to be together, but I think the decision to do the textbook depended upon what Pat said [...] our feeling like we could trust each other and [...] could let each other revise. [...] we both didn't especially like textbooks and yet we saw so many people use textbooks. And so we said, "Why don't we do one?" So in a sense, we set out to create something in a genre that [...] we had negative feelings about [...]. The decision to write together came from wanting to produce one of these things, and well, clearly, I couldn't do it alone, and [...] we wanted to have a textbook that embodied our take on writing.

PETER.   [...] I actually think we came up with a method that was not so wasteful of time. We would each start a new section and each start a different one and then just trade disks and take it over. So we spent very little time doing what I think is most frustrating sitting in a room, arguing about a phrase or a clause.

PAT.   [...] the first semester when I was at Stony Brook, I sat in on the practicum, which Peter was teaching. And I think that there was a lot of conversation and talk [...] and I think that that probably had a lot to do with our being able to see how each other thought.

PETER.   The role Pat played back then was fairly often to be quarrelsome. And right from the beginning was very helpful and actually a relief to me. [...] And it led to this feeling that we can collaborate, and we don't have to agree—that each person can go where they're going, and that's not a problem; in fact, it's an advantage.

PAT.   I was trying to think back to the whole thing of conversation, and it seems to me that, obviously, we talked all the time. But [...] it wasn't necessarily that it was focused on the textbook as such. [...] I think the conversation and talk was like the bedrock on which the book was built. [...] But [...] I just don't remember a whole heck of a lot of talk. We traded the disks, and we'd write comments to each other. [...] And if one of us was going to do something fairly radical, I think we checked that out, but otherwise, we just sort of went along.

PETER.   [...]. When we're in the same program, when we're working together on the same project, I think the conversations happen, but we don't even remember them [...] as far as [...] revision, what I really find most precious this crudely simple method where one person starts it and the other person takes the disk and just does it [...] the start is very primitive; the revision is very major. But then when it goes back to the first person, that person might make nontrivial changes [...] and there, too, we didn't talk about it. We just maltreated each other's text.

PAT.   [...] we're doing this brief edition [...] and I think I wrote Peter a message that said, "This sounds like a new book; I'm getting concerned; I don't know about this." And Peter sort of brushed it off, and then about a week and a half later, he sent this memo that was totally un-Peter-like which said something to the effect to the editor we keep saying, don't do x and you continue to do x! And I [...] realized again that we were on the same wavelength.

PETER.   I'd internalized what you'd said.

PAT.   Yes, I mean, you just sort of brushed it off at first and I thought, "Oh, maybe it just doesn't concern Peter," and then a week and a half later, I see this memo [...] that made the statements much more strongly than I had made them. [...] I remember the first time Peter gave me a draft of something I was totally shocked because I would never have given anybody something that looked like [it] [...] it was disorganized [...]. It had no beginning, middle, and end. It was reflective; it would say something like, "Well, I don't know if I really want to say this." [...] And the language tended to be sort of colloquial and off-hand [...]. I certainly would never have given anybody anything in my writing that looked like that. On the other hand, the writing that I gave him was far more academic. [...] sentences up to 150 words long [...] And I think this drove Peter nuts. So while I was dealing with his mess, he's there trying to break my sentences up. [...] So I think that our styles were really very different, and I certainly know that I have moved toward Peter's end of it. Even when I write alone now, I know that the lessons we actually made or that I'm writing actually work.

PETER.   In a way, I don't want to draw a conclusion that you can only write collaboratively with people that you trust, but where there is a sense of complete trust, [it works].

PAT.   [...] and I think that trust is not only about the ideas that we have but also somehow the willingness to trust each other's language in the way of saying things. [...] I hear Peter's voice often. Particularly [...] when I'm working with a tangled sentence, and I realize that it's one of those things that in the past, I would have tried to develop some sort of complicated syntax to deal with the idea, and then I hear Peter's voice, and I realize that what I need to do is break it down [...]. I was doing something, I've forgotten what it was, that I was in charge of [...] I really feel like he was taking it over and doing it, so I was really very annoyed. [...] I wanted to reclaim it back again, I think, so I started to do a rewrite, and I wanted to reclaim it, but I also wanted to include what he wanted to do. And so I started out revising with both of those goals in mind, and what I realized, of course, is that both the goals disappeared, and that [...]. I somehow ended up with something that was not what I started with and not what he suggested, but it was [...]

a much, much, much firmer unit and chapter than it would have been [...] and I think that's when I got a real lesson in collaborative writing. And like Peter now, I don't write anything without showing it to somebody.

PETER.   In a way we've gotten under each other's skin as far as even our thinking. So again, it's a little rare to build up that trust, and working together created that trust.

PAT.   As far as the creative tensions were concerned, I think that they were just productive like the story I just told.

PETER.   The way in which Pat would disagree with me is somehow key. It's interesting that when someone disagrees with you, and some of them were very fundamental, the disagreements [...] that you had a way of being completely clear about it completely open, not beating around the bush in such a way that somehow it made it very easy for me to listen. In other words, sometimes people disagree with you and you want to fight them. [...] But [...] with Pat, [...] the disagreements were just naked and out there and yet able to be dealt with. And they would lead somewhere.

PAT.   But [...] they were never personal [...] I mean, the personal was important to both of us, so the discussions [...] never got to be like a personal thing.

PETER.   [...] the ground of all this was a very personal relationship, and yet it wasn't personal.

PAT.   And you asked about the ownership of language and ideas, and in some ways our collaboration may be different than other people's because Peter's ideas were already well-known. And I know that Peter owns freewriting, and I know that he owns the doubting and believing game, and I've really never felt any ownership of those ideas. But I feel like I'm inside them so thoroughly that I can write as though they're mine. And Peter never really claimed ownership of them. It's just something that we just sort of all know. And I think that [in] the textbook now, the thing that he can most find ownership [of] [...] is the unit on voice. [...] But when I reread the [textbook] [...] look back at some of the things we've written in the past, some things will jump out and I know they're mine. [...] maybe sometimes it's just a phrase or something. And sometimes it'll jump out, and I know it's his. I'll say, "That's a Peter-ism or something." And a lot of it I just can't pigeon-hole. I have no idea who wrote it.

PETER.   That's exactly it. Every now and then, it's hers or mine, but a lot of it is ours.

PAT.   But at one point early in my career, one of my former mentors said to me "You have to make sure you don't just become Peter Elbow's shadow." [...] I hadn't thought about it before and I certainly didn't want to be a shadow. [...] [when I was] up for promotion [...] one of the notes I got back when I handed in the file was that they wanted from the third edition of the textbook some idea of what I was responsible for. [...] interestingly enough, when I came up for tenure, even though I had those collaborative things, but I don't remember them asking that question of me. But this time I got a specific question: "Can I identify what in the textbook is mine?"

Time for Reflection

What did you hear Peter and Pat saying about trust and ownership in their collaborative partnership? What other questions about their writing together did this excerpt from their interview make you want to ask them?

Cy Knoblauch and Lil Brannon

Cy Knoblauch and Lil Brannon shared their perceptions about writing collaboratively with us in an e-mail exchange. They have coauthored several books and articles, both teach at UNC Charlotte, and, unlike the other authors whose voices we heard, they are married.

CY.   First, I should say that each of us has worked on collaborative projects that did not include the other. [...] I think collaboration in our field is popular, to a degree, simply because of the range of disciplines incorporated under the aegis of composition studies and therefore the range of opportunities for cross-disciplinary thinking. I once did an essay with Peter Johnston that depended on a blend of his work in reading theory and educational psychology and my work in literary and rhetorical theory. [...] We found it beneficial to leverage new thinking through the complementarity and conflict of views.

LIL.   Collaboration also comes about because those who teach writing are working on a common enterprise. The problems in teaching are very complex and interesting, so discussions with colleagues are often purposeful, rich, and exciting. It is usually out of this talk that collaborative projects come about.

CY.   Lil and I started writing together when we were running the writing program (with Paula Johnson) at NYU in the early '80s. Proximity was obviously an advantage, but between us we've worked with many colleagues who would not have been suitable writing partners. In our case, what has made writing together a productive experience is the fact that we share similar attitudes and points of view about teaching and composition theory while coming from provocatively different academic backgrounds. We start in different places conceptually but nearly always meet at the far end of our lines of thinking. Lil is a true composition specialist from one of the first graduate programs—East Texas—to recognize the field. I consider myself primarily a theorist in language and rhetoric, with a background in classical as well as English literatures tempered by the "semiotics" emphasis that Bob Scholes was introducing at Brown around the time I was there as a graduate student. I got into composition studies by accident when asked to run the writing program at Columbia after having been hired there as an 18th-century British lit. specialist. [...] my interest was real enough, and by the time I got to NYU, I was an experienced WPA . We worked with Nancy Sommers for awhile there on issues of response to student writing and learned a lot from that experience about our different but complementary vantage points. We wrote a couple of articles based on that research, which set the stage for the book projects that we did subsequently. We've been collaborating ever since, although we have also done a good bit of writing on our own.

LIL.   I began collaborating on projects while working on my doctorate. My first collaborative essay was written with Jeanette Harris for the *Journal of Basic Writing.* [...] When I finished graduate school, I took a position at UNC-Wilmington and was hired at the same time that John Clifford was hired. As the two new compositionists, we had much to talk about, and out of that talk came several articles. It was also during this time that I met Steve North at CCCCs, and we decided to invent and collaborative[ly] work on *The Writing Center Journal.* When I moved to New York and began working with Cy, Paula, and Nancy, collaboration seemed "natural."

LIL and CY.   We would say that talk in the early stages of conceptualization, and in between drafts of actual texts, is absolutely crucial. Indeed, it is the essence of our collaboration—because our writing habits couldn't be more different. [...] Through talk, we get a feel for each other's positions, take advantage of each other's arguments and insights, exchange source materials from our different academic backgrounds, and steer each other out of impasses and away from intellectual blind spots. We absorb the results of this interplay before much writing actually takes place, knowing that the writing itself will necessarily depend more on one of us than the other and knowing that our ways of fashioning prose do not mesh well enough to allow for that more local kind of talk related to the tactics of organizing a text.

CY.   We have never been able to sit down, pen in hand, and cooperate in drafting one sentence, then the next. Lil is an Elbovian, freewriting, cooking-and-growing, writing-center, writing-group, multiple-drafting evacuator of prose, who needs to shape her thinking at every stage by writing it down. I'm a hopelessly linear, relentlessly rationalist nitpicker who will never allow a sentence to stand provisionally, let alone a paragraph or a page, until—at least for the moment—I really believe I can live with it. I can't look at Lil's early prose without experiencing mental sea-sickness—she, following Ann Berthoff, has "learned the uses of chaos." I am constitutionally unsuited to chaos. I see organization in my head and realize it, with grim determination, one sentence at a time—revising, to be sure, but in the way a sculptor chisels, bit by bit, until a satisfactory form emerges.

LIL.   When Cy writes the first draft, it is very difficult for him to change anything. [...] So we have to do a lot of talk and planning and thinking before he begins writing, or I have to write the first draft.

CY.   The good news about this fundamental difference of style is that Lil can pull me out of the tunnel vision that linear thinkers get themselves into, while I can cut to the chase when Lil is still hip deep in unfocused prose. But it's also fair to say that, for us, "revision" may be a little too narrow a concept with which to describe our collaborative give and take. We will certainly go back to the drawing board in response to each other's questions, challenges, disagreements. But we work mainly on the "macro" level. We won't usually tussle over *this* word or *that* sentence (a focus that would invariably come way too early for Lil and way too late for me). If we're satisfied that the gist of a piece is what we were looking for, that counts as closure (although the writing will occasionally suggest new possibilities, in which case we'll talk them out).

CY and LIL.   We don't write differently because we're collaborating, but we do anticipate a more immediate—and in a sense compulsory—obligation to revise if we're not seeing eye to eye. We have even abandoned some projects because of our differences on the issues.

CY.   In a sense, writing "alone" is my normal condition even when collaborating. I'm less dependent on feedback, in general, than Lil is.

The benefits of collaboration are truly substantial, and so I accept the accommodations that go along with that arrangement. But I don't do it (as Lil perhaps does) because it fits comfortably with my temperament or my habits as a writer.

LIL.   I would rather collaborate than write alone, though I find myself writing alone a lot. Writing alone is easier in many ways: it takes less time for one thing. When I write alone, I am always asking for response to my work either from Cy or from colleagues. I need to know directly the impact of my words on others. Cy writes a paper and only as an afterthought asks me what I make of it. When we collaborate we talk about our ideas more. It matters that we agree about what we say.

LIL.   When we first started writing together, we decided whose name would go first by who typed the final draft. After our first book we bought our first computer together. The drudgery of typing did not work then for placing our names on articles. I'm not sure now how we decided to go with Knoblauch and Brannon, but at some point we thought it best just to stick with one way of referring to ourselves. After we finished our first book project, we did not collaborate together for many years. We got married during that time, and we knew how much time and concentration such projects take. We worked alone so that we could live our lives. But after awhile (I guess one might call it selective amnesia), we decided we would write one article together. That article went well, so we decided to try another. After awhile we could see the outline of a book, and before we knew it we were working on *Critical Teaching and the Idea of Literacy*. It has been several years since that book was published, and only this year have we begun to collaborate on an article together.

CY.   I suppose I've taken the scribal lead in much of our collaborative writing [...] because it suits my obsessively tidy, nitpicking mind to work out the small stuff. But that doesn't count for us as a measure of ownership—it's simply a convenient division of labor, like sharing housework [...] we long ago faced a hard fact—that absolute ego corrupts absolutely. We simply don't keep score when we're collaborating. Once you do, it's time to find another way of working.

LIL.   I have to feel sure that I am in the writing, so after our long conversations, I often write letters to Cy (I call them first drafts), but they take the shape of letters and notes so that Cy is working from my impressions of our conversations.

CY.   [...] given the nature of our collaboration, it isn't as necessary to be sitting at the same table in order to proceed.

LIL.   I'm not sure that living together makes collaboration easier either. In fact, it may make it more difficult precisely because it can take over your life. We do not have a place to retreat to or a disinterested partner. Cy knows when I'm reading or grading papers or at the gym. I know when he is on the golf course or watching football. We can't invent an excuse for why something is not done.

Time for Reflection

What did you learn from Cy and Lil's e-mail responses about proximity and personal connection in their experiences of writing with each other? What other questions do you want to ask them?

Peter Mortensen and Janet Carey Eldred

Janet Carey Eldred and Peter Mortensen talked with us at CCCC in April 2000, about their collaborative writing partnership, which began when they were assistant professors at the University of Kentucky with an article entitled "Reading Literacy Narratives" for *College English* in 1992. They focused in the interview on how their archival research turned into a collaboratively authored monograph on rhetoric and literacy entitled *Imagining Rhetoric: Composing Women of the Early United States*, and published by Pittsburgh University Press in 2002.

JANET.   And it was just a thing where I said "Wow! We're doing some of the same stuff." I don't remember, maybe Peter does, of how we got hooked on *Pygmalion*. [...] I have no memory of how we initially decided to do it. I remember us working together, but honestly [...] [it felt] like one minute we were writing and the next [we were in print]. And that was our first collaborative effort.

PETER.   My recollection at the beginning was that you put something under my door. You xeroxed an article about something and wrote a note on it, and that's how we got started, and we spent a lot of time talking about literacy. [...] Once we'd finished the literacy narrative, we quickly thought about moving on to [...] [archival work related to the boarding school]. [...] a senior member of the department, [...] sort of turned us on to this collection of early American titles that nobody had looked at.

JANET.   We had him for lunch at my house. [...] a long, kind of working lunch where he trained us on what the stuff was and where we should go and what we should do.

PETER.   The project that we're finishing up now really [...] wouldn't be in its current form right now if [...].

JANET.   Except that there's another part of that, which is that Peter has that strong interest in work in the local archives, and so at the same time that we were working on the stuff that Don had told us about and kind of focused us and gotten us going in that direction, I think that it was really retraining in a way, I mean giving us a little seminar. And at the same time Peter was really doing local archives [...] and then we started looking at other local archives, and we ended up not pursuing that as much as we thought we would.

PETER.   We did a lot of transcription not knowing exactly what we were going to do with it [...] and we ended up passing that along to one of our graduate students, who was [...].

JANET.   [...] just now finishing up graduate school. [...] but, the main thing was, and this is really crucial, I think, the main reason we didn't pursue the archival work was, plain and simply, was children. [...] We used to be able to drive somewhere and spend all day transcribing and filing through archives, and then we ended up with kids. Separately. And a lot's changed, and it's affected our research. But I think, in a way, that's good. The book was very unfocused, and it was huge. And the work that we ended up doing, I think, needed to be done, and was valuable and more focused, so I'm not sorry that it went in that direction.

PETER.   No, not at all.

JANET.   [When we sit down to write together], we make sentences. We're both, I think, resistant starters [...] our normal process would be to put off the starting of it endlessly. [...] There's always more research you can do. [...] we just kind of sat down, and time got tighter and tighter with kids.

PETER.   So it was like 9 to 2 on Fridays, once a week.

JANET.   And I can't live without food. So [...] we'd get started, and [...] in the middle of the day [...] we had to plan on food. So it left us very little time to actually do the writing, and so what we would say was, 'OK, make sentences. We can always revise then.' So that during these times we had to make sentences so that we could go to lunch and then read what we did for the day.

PETER.   One person would be keying in, but we would swap off.

JANET.   Week by week we would just start with maybe what we had, and then [...].

PETER.   We published articles, so we did the beginning of the book in three chunks. There was a piece in *Rhetoric Society Quarterly,* a piece in *Rhetoric Review.* Both of those got really radically revised and incorporated into the book manuscript.

JANET.   [...] as we've completed the book now and are waiting on revision, it's very useful that parts of it have already been reviewed so that we've gotten feedback in the early stages. [...] part of the reason for doing articles is for merit review. [...] one way for sure to get salary depression is to be working on a book that you don't publish any part of [...] and we put out articles in effect so that we could have some line for our merit review period.

PETER.   After July of 1999, we did work separately, more or less. [...] [because] I moved to Illinois.

JANET.   We were real focused. We knew what method [...]. And that was useful when we did have to write separately because we didn't have to do any more searching for what the research method was, what the ground was, what the process was. We had all that, and so, when we went to write that last chapter, we knew exactly what we needed to accomplish, and it was a little easier for us to farm it out. And, if I remember right, what we would do is, we had opposite days of work. [...] So Peter would work on Tuesday, and I would work on Friday, and we did the thing where I would work and ship it to him, and then he would work and ship it back to me. [...] There's one question I wanted to talk about because just the very phrasing of it made me laugh, and it was the one that was 'How does writing collaboratively help you sustain response and revision, prolong your composing process, and resist closure?' And I can tell you that I have never had any problem resisting closure, and nor has Peter. Out problem, the thing that collaboration did for us, was to force us to close because there would be the two of us and we would say, OK [...] On this date this is what we will have done.

PETER.   I think pre-tenure, actually, we had less trouble. There was a clear reason to get this stuff done [...].

Time for Reflection

How do Peter and Janet's concerns and patterns of collaboration differ from Peter and Pat's, from Cy and Lil's? What more would you like to know about how Peter's move has affected their collaborative writing?

Kate Ronald and Hephzibah Roskelly

Kate Ronald and Hephzibah Roskelly also met with us at CCCC in April 2000, in Minneapolis. Over breakfast, we talked with them about their collaborative history as graduate students, administrators, conference presenters, and coauthors of *Reason to Believe: Romanticism, Pragmatism, and the Teaching of Writing*.

HEPSIE.   We were assistant directors of comp. together. And we hadn't known each other before that very well. Kate had been down in the Writing Center, which was, of course, then called writing lab, and she was diagnosing all over the place for [. . .], and I really was in creative writing. And so that really was sort of never the twain shall meet. But the person who was the director of comp, Joseph Comprone, put us together. And really that was the beginning of what we mean by collaboration because we did everything together. We did the schedule together; we taught as TAs together; we did workshops together. We really figured out how to stand in front of a room and talk together.

KATE.   It wasn't conscious. We didn't sit down and say that we're going to do these things together. It's just that it happened. We're going to administer together [. . .].

HEPSIE.   But of course the truth is that if it hadn't been that it clicked, we wouldn't have continue in that way. There are a lot of people who administer together who don't [collaborate]. It divides up your time. OK, I'll be in the office on Tuesday and Thursday, and you be Monday, Wednesday, and Friday. There are a lot of people who do that, and it's perfectly easy to handle it that way. Kate and I never did that. We were in the office together all the time. But I think we learned just about how we clicked very early, and so we kept doing it that way. [. . .] [So as graduate students] we were talking together, and [. . .] in the writing center, we team taught. And that was another way that we learned our own timing really quickly. [. . .] And so when we started writing together, it really wasn't a big wrench for us to figure out how to do it. Because we knew each other, trusted each other, had heard each other's words so much that [. . .].

KATE.   And read each other's writing.

HEPSIE.   And read each other's writing. I mean, Kate was my first reader for pieces of the dissertation, as I was hers. So we knew enough that when we started writing, it wasn't hard to do. But the impulse to write together was not, "Hey, you've got this great idea; let's publish it." It was very personal. It was, we want to find a way to stay together, and it we're both going to stay in this crazy profession, the way to do it is to write together. And that'll give us an excuse to find ways to be together and so we'll always have that that we can use. I mean, that really was the impulse.

KATE.   I think a big part of our collaborative story is that we were in many ways very unprofessional. Very unprofessional as writers and graduate students. In fact it was quite a shock to us when we realized the our success in graduate school, getting the degree, meant that we would have to leave each other.

HEPSIE.   I know that sounds really stupid.

KATE.   It sounds ridiculous.

HEPSIE.   But it was a shock.

KATE.   And we managed to bring ourselves about at far apart as we could, to Nebraska and Boston. And so the first time we wrote together for publication, the first time we presented together, was really an attempt to keep working together [...] [T]he thing a writer needs is an audience who believes in you to listen to what you have to say. Now, having written with Hephsie for all these years, she's in my head. And so, her voice, "Yes, you can do this. You're good. You're clever. You're smart," is right there next to that little editor that says, "You can't do this," And that, to me, is an amazing benefit of collaboration. And stylistically, I've learn a lot from Hephsie.

HEPSIE.   We've both learned a lot.

KATE.   [...] we got this piece coming out in a collection on personal scholarship, and we each did a little part of it where we were talking about what we'd learned. And the theme of it was Hephsie talking about my making her go deeper and take more care, and my talking about her making me think about the metaphor I've used, and of course, she does love to stop and look at historical markers. Like when you're on the road. And I just want to get there, I don't care [...]. But as a writer she makes me go down side roads that I normally wouldn't go down, and she makes me look in odd places. [...] I'm the organized one. I manage the disks. I will make sure that there's a bibliography that actually has the right format.

HEPSIE.   I'm a much better solitary writer now than I would have been had I never collaborated. I mean it just—you develop as an individual out of a social relationship that you find. That's how people learn. And collaboration is an instant proof of the way the social construction theory works.

KATE.   I tell all my graduate students, women particularly, that my best piece of advice as a mentor is that you've got to find somebody to go through this with, somebody you trust. Somebody to talk to about all of the pain and the competition and all the tests. Because I think that in general it's quite a competitive environment, and the best thing you could do for yourself is to find yourself a friend to go through it with. I would wish for all my graduate students the kind of experience we had in grad. school. And I know they're not all having it. [...] Some of my graduate students have collaborative, but I've never structured that into anything. I've never made anybody do that.

HEPSIE.   I [...] encourage [my graduate students] to collaborate. I teach a course, and it really came about in great measure because of our collaboration. I teach a course about the social construction of varying collaborations. And in that course, they have to collaborate in any number of ways. They have to do group stuff. I [began the course by writing] a little about my collaboration with Kate. I sometimes give them a little draft of something we're working on. I do something to help them see the connection that I'm making between the theory we're reading and what I do as a writer. And my student are doing a lot of collaborative work [...] in terms of making presentations, thinking of their work together when they go to conferences, playing off of one another [...] not only do we need to demystify with graduate students the processes of what we do, but we need to theorize what we do. [...] and so when I teach that course in collaboration, and I'm teaching theory about how people learn, I'm putting it to the test of process with my own work, and I'm showing them that that test of process has consequences in the way we read that theory.

Time for Reflection

Why is personal connection so important to Kate and Hepsie as they describe their motivations for and habits of writing together? Is their partnership different from others you've read about because they're women? How do you think gender influences the writing habits of collaborative pairs?

Hans Ostrom and Wendy Bishop

Hans Ostrom and Wendy Bishop replied to our request for an interview through a single e-mail response that they created jointly, in a back-and-forth way. They share information about their beginnings as collaborative writers and some of their experiences writing textbooks and poems together.

WENDY.   I guess we decided [to collaborate] when we re-met in Seattle at the 1989, CCCC after not seeing each other since leaving Davis, CA. M.A. grad. school and found we'd been doing the same sorts of things—teaching writing and creative writing and asking questions about those fields and about the profession. I know it was [Hans'] statement: let's do something together. In fact, [he'll] often say that, just that: let's do something together. Which always means: let's write something together. Oddly, for us, I think the very act of talking about almost any subject strikes such a cord of wacky congruence that we both want to (a) write and (b) write together. After the first time, it proved soooo fun, that it was easy for me to say so too, just as often: what should we do next started to replace, let's do something together.

HANS.   Yes, in undergraduate school at Davis, we used to meet with one other student sometimes after the poetry workshop with Karl Shapiro. We'd trade drafts, etc. Then the reconnection in 1989, Seattle CCCC. By hook or crook, temperament and/or experience, we seem to have so much in common as writers and teachers. We traverse boundaries of genre, of "scholar," "poet," writer, teacher. We are interested in interrogating boundaries in English studies. Besides this shared "vision" (too pretentious a word), we have a laconic affect, I'd say-a Why Not? Attitude toward projects, authorship, etc. I'm not exactly sure why, but from the first we seemed to set egos aside or, more accurately maybe, just always find ways to mesh egos. We've found the collaborative writing pleasurable, too. I feel that, when I collaborate with [Wendy], I will often write something different or better or both than I would have on my own. There's an enormous sense of possibility regardless of the genre into which we are about to travel.

WENDY.   [...] [Now] we meet at conferences mainly [...] and we talk about what we've seen at the conference and what entertains us, drives us nuts and what we wish someone was doing and invariably one of us says: we could do that. We spent that time, second meeting, in Chicago walking around the booksellers exhibits learning how to talk to the publishers. Balancing a funny idea between us and pitching it. It was a strange new world to me and I wouldn't have walked around without [Hans], not just [his] experience having done lit. and textbook publishing. But [his] sense of humor and to hell with them (or it)—let's try it. For a shy person [he] loaned me a supreme momentary self-confidence—or the playful "what if" and "why not" conversation did. The sense that there's nothing to lose and we'd already lost out in the main—literature branch—lottery of English departments led me to feel a wonderful sassy freedom to think, talk, eventually write broadly. We gave each other permission in those conversations.

HANS.   Probably an observer would say [Wendy] and I converse surprisingly little. We both have private personae rather different from our teaching personae, don't we? Meaning we're relatively reserved, laid-back, and laconic in day-to-day conversations even if we've developed more performance-oriented (too strong a term) personae for the class. At any rate, at conferences we just walk around and mumble about everything and then slide into conversations about projects. Like most long-time colleagues, we have a short-hand "code" talk-yes? I remember so many conversations about a project where it's "mumble, mumble, mumble" and then "okay, then, let's do that," and we've sorted out a fairly major wrinkle, problem, task. We hardly ever argue or debate when we disagree because who cares who wins? [...] we just up-front give each other permission to "write over" each other's drafts. With [*Metro*] there were so many drafts of a couple of collaboratively written exercises that I quite literally forgot who wrote what sometimes although since I was so-called "lead" editor, I read so much manuscript so many times that that contributed to the blurring. I can't explain fully why we're so comparatively ego-less when we collaborate-especially when in other spheres we have "plenty ego!" I guess there's this sense that it's the work that counts—we're producing something, so "whatever works, works." [...] the work is the thing when we work together. It probably helps that we have substantial "solo careers." That is, I wonder about people who collaborate so much that they start to get nervous about "authority" & then insecurity builds and things fall apart. A Lennon/McCartney deal. But mainly I like watching how Wendy improves my writing when she changes it. Writers like seeing writing made better.

WENDY.   Early on I realized we were doing this "write-over" and it amazed, pleased me and then became normal. My base-line expectation for writing. Perhaps because we *began* writing over with some poems, we got through the worst of the ego issues without noticing it since poetry seems the most resistant genre for this [...] When we quickly moved to co-editing a collection and coauthoring a talk/essay or two, the writing across seemed very comfortable. Did it matter so much if he changed my phrase when he was changing my punctuation? No, both made it better since we were sometimes doing dialogue—as here—the next move to smoothing out dialogue was to merge the voices [...]. I can now assign myself to "write like Hans" to get out of a drafting spot and it's wonderfully freeing—I can import what I imagine to be his more than my "to hell with the audience" approach and break through some useless propriety.

HANS.   In terms of process, I doubt if we've changed each other all that much—I'm talking about the basic day-to-day habits of a writer. What's interesting to me is that the personal habits have little if any negative effect on our collaborations. The influence for me comes when I write poems or criticism or scholarly things alone—I know darn well I've picked up perspectives via osmosis from you-ideas, habits of experimentation, rhetorical moves.

WENDY.   Since I learn by having written and I love to learn, I need to keep writing and finishing so that small learnings add up to bigger learnings, life-long learnings. and as I've said, learning from Hans' insights—a caring co-thinker—is one of the greatest pleasures in the world. Can I learn from others: journals, friends, writers, thinkers? Of course, do and can and will. but there's something about Hans' vocabulary that is very palatable for me: it involves an immense amount of word play at the sentence level and a lack of (often a making fun of) jargon that lets the ideas show in ways I need as a thinker. In a way, he gives me what I need, distills—I'm thinking here of the intro to [Colors] which he first drafted. Actually, I find myself sometimes dismantling those very things—I think I some-times then think of "other readers" and translate Hans' play into something a little less facetious when I draft, add a few connectives, take out a pun. He's a terrific outliner too—where I can get bogged in working an idea out at the paragraph/section level, he can scan and then take out a pen and re-outline a project. Even though I'm the "squawk-talker" in person and he's quiet—I see him as being more radical in drafts and I'm sometimes the clean up crew or the one who says—well we could but we probably shouldn't do that. I may have more of an eye toward audience. Maybe that's why I'm a more extensive reviser. We're both sloppy. But Hans is sloppy because he's a fewer drafts person and on to the next project. I'm sloppy cuz I gnaw bigger patches of text to death but then get too exhausted to edit well and he can come in and find my simple errors like a clerk 'tsking at the mess I've made. though he doesn't much like to and we'd both prefer to be copy edited by a really fine copy-editor (obviously we've sometimes had less than fine ones). We're hard to edit though because we both push alt[ernative] style a lot. I'd say our alt[ternative] style play—the way we read each other's drafts may actually *be* our talk, the way we talk to each other [. . .].

PROCESS CODA (WENDY and HANS).   Wendy was sent the request to write on this subject. She forwarded the request to Hans and said she'd only do it if he agreed. Hans agreed because he thought it would be a good excuse to think about writing together—to get in work gear and work up a project. When he said yes, Wendy only said yes too after thinking that heck—yes, work together, we like that, and: we should send this to a journal too if it goes well. That is, as soon as it became a collaborative project it *became* interesting. And then our self-interview took place in three e-mail exchanges (if phone interview had been a requirement, one of us at least guesses it wouldn't have happened at all): Wendy wrote answers to several questions between classes and ran out of time. Hans answered and continued (ditto the out of time). Wendy wrote back and extended. Clean up. Reread. Learn. If it had taken more than that; we'd not have done it. To do it with less than all our energies, though, would have been impossibly unlike us. We looked forward to reading each other, to the returned text. One last re-read reminded us to add that contrary to what it sounds like, we do value other things: families, gardening, teaching writing, videos, reading, traveling, eating are some of those things (and writing poetry because "it is there."). But, there isn't a time, either, when learning about writing can't arrest us in mid-tracks, pre-occupy our minds all day/night until, there, we have to say and see what we've said. At the end of this warm-up, we've started exchanging e-mails about the next project. This time we'll write the book and then find the publisher (our way to deal with the problems we've been encountering that chip away at enthusiasm). So thank you. And you can decide if just one of us or both of us (or neither of us) wrote this last word.

Time for Reflection

What are some of the most striking aspects of Wendy and Hans's approach to collaborative writing? What does their distinctive use of e-mail tell you about their ideas about collaboration? What do you make of their "process coda"?

How Might the Conversation Continue?

There will always be professional writers who refuse to talk about the way they write, why they write, or what they intend to accomplish by writing. These writers strongly believe in the highly personal or even magical quality of the writing process, one that is either unspeakable in its mystery or easily jinxed. Fortunately for us, these ten writers whose words you've just read believe strongly in the importance of talking about writing. All teachers themselves, they know how much others can learn from listening to stories. They also know that because each one of us brings to the stories his or her own set of personal experiences and histories, we each intersect with the stories differently. Indeed, these differences, this personal intersection is the heart of collaboration as we've described it.

Trying Out Collaborative Writing

I. Insert yourself into the conversations that these collaborative pairs have had. Using the questions you have generated in the "Time for Reflection" sections of this chapter as a starting place, create a dialogue among all the writers and yourself. What questions would they ask one another? What questions would you ask individuals or pairs of writers? How might you expect them to respond? And how might you respond?

II. Although we've emphasized the relationship these five pairs of writers have as coauthors, each of them writes and publishes singly as well. Find an article or book chapter or book excerpt written by one of these collaborative pairs and an article written by one or both of them solo. How would you describe the differences in voice/style/subject matter between the solo writing and the collaborative writing? Team up with a writing partner to do this analysis. Be sure to discuss the collaborative process you will use in order to accomplish this task.

Works Cited

Ashton-Jones, Evelyn, and Dene Kay Thomas. "Composition, Collaboration, and Women's Ways of Knowing: A Conversation with Mary Belenky." *(Interviews): Cross-Disciplinary Perspectives on*

Rhetoric and Literacy. Ed. Gary A. Olson, and Irene Gale.
    Carbondale: Southern Illinois UP, 1991. 27–44.
Bishop, Wendy, and Hans Ostrom. E-mail. 27 September 2000.
Blythe, Hal, and Charlie Sweet. "Collaborwriting." *Writers on Writing.*
    Ed. Tom Waldrep. New York: Random House, 1985. 39–43.
Collaborate! www.stanford.edu/group/collaborate/.
Day, Kami, and Michele Eodice. *(First Person)²: A Study of Coauthoring
    in the Academy.* Logan: Utah State UP, 2001.
Ede, Lisa, and Andrea A. Lunsford. "Collaboration and Concepts of
    Authorship." *PMLA* 116.2 (2001): 354–69.
——. *Singular Texts/Plural Authors: Perspectives on Collaborative Writing.*
    Carbondale: Southern Illinois UP, 1990.
Elbow, Peter, and Pat Belanoff. Telephone Interview. 1 May 2000.
Freire, Paulo. *The Pedagogy of the Oppressed.* New York: Continuum, 1986.
Knoblauch, Cy, and Lil Brannon. E-mail. 20 February 2001.
Mortensen, Peter, and Janet Carey Eldred. Personal Interview.
    15 April 2000.
Ronald, Kate, and Hephzibah Roskelly. Personal Interview. 14 April 2000.
——. "Women Taking Students Seriously." Conference on College
    Composition and Communication, Minneapolis, MN, 13 April 2000.

For Further Reading

Anson, Chris, Laura Brady, and Marion Larson. "Collaboration in
    Practice." *Writing on the Edge* 4.2 (Spring 1993): 80–96.
Hutcheon, Linda, and Michael Hutcheon. "A Convenience of Marriage:
    Collaboration and Interdisciplinarity." *PMLA* 116.5 (October 2001):
    1364–76.
John-Steiner, Vera. *Creative Collaboration.* New York and London: Oxford
    UP, 2000.
Leonardi, Susan J., and Rebecca A. Pope. "(Co)Labored Li(v)es; or,
    Love's Labors Queered." *PMLA* 116.3 (May 2001): 631–37.
Lunsford, Andrea A., and Lisa Ede. "Collaboration and Compromise:
    The Fine Art of Writing with a Friend." *Writers on Writing.*
    Volume II. Ed. Tom Waldrep. New York: Random House, 1988.
    121–27.
Monseau, Virginia R., Jeanne M. Gerlach, and Lisa J. McClure. "The
    Making of a Book: A Collaboration of Writing, Responding, and
    Revising." Ed. Sally Barr Reagan, Thomas Fox, and David Bleich.

Writing With: New Directions in Collaborative Teaching, Learning, and Research. Albany: State U of New York P, 1994. 61–75.

Ronald, Kate, and Hephzibah Roskelly. "Learning to Take It Personally." *Personal Effects: The Social Character of Scholarly Writing.* Ed. Deborah H. Holdstein, and David Bleich. Logan: Utah State UP, 2001. 253–66.

Yancey, Kathleen, and Michael Spooner. "A Single Good Mind: Collaboration, Cooperation, and the Writing Self." *College Composition and Communication* 49.1 (February 1998): 45–63.

Afterword: Am I Ready to Write Collaboratively?

In the Preface, we promised that by reading this book, you'd learn a lot about Composition in the context of what we had to say about collaborative writing. And so you have read about the structure of knowledge and language, the elasticity of the writing process, the importance of conversation for coauthors, writers' struggles with authorial identity and textual ownership, and the complexity of disciplinary and departmental politics. Now, having read, considered, and discussed all of that, it's time to ask yourself, "Am I ready to write collaboratively?" and then to engage with another writer in a final collaborative research/writing activity, one that is more extensive than the ones that you've tried out so far.

In order to help you answer that question and to increase the chances that your first experiences of writing with another author are positive, we have put together the following list of questions for you to consider as you contemplate entering into a partnership with another writer. You'll probably recognize the questions as emerging from the topics of the chapters that you have read. We recommend that you go through these questions in two ways: (1) by yourself, and (2) together with another writer. That is, to be ready to write collaboratively isn't just about whether you as an individual are ready to go; it's also about whether another writer and you are ready together. While it is very important that you engage in honest self-reflection about your writing habits and expectations, it is also important that, as the first step in what might become a long collaborative journey, you recognize the pleasure of working with another writer. For when the article is done or the book is on the shelf, what remains for all of us who write together is the memory of having created something together that we could not have done alone, having enjoyed writing, talking, rewriting, agreeing, disagreeing, laughing, and struggling with another writer.

Shared Thoughts About Writing and Thinking

- What ideas about writing, teaching, and the way ideas come to be do you and your coauthor share? Where do you have differences?

Finding Out What You Have in Common

- If you and your coauthor were to sit down over a cup of coffee, what would you talk about? What topics of conversation would most likely come up between you?
- Can you imagine having a conversation with your prospective coauthor about ideas that matter to you and about which you feel both protective and insecure?
- In what setting did you and your coauthor meet? How long have you known one another? Have you ever exchanged ideas or drafts with one another?
- Why do you want to write together?

Looking at How You Write Alone and Imagining How You Will Write Together

- In what ways do you expect you will have to change or adapt your typical composing habits or writing style in order to write together?
- What kinds of practices do you currently engage in during composing alone that you might see as being preliminary or preparatory to writing with someone? Peer review? Asking readers for their feedback? Being a reader for other writers?

Reflecting on the Way that Others Influence Your Work and Self-image

- Has either of you ever written with another writer? Were your experiences successful or not? How do you explain their success or failure?
- Have you ever worked with any one individual over a long period of time? How did the relationship between you change and grow?
- Are you willing to revise? Do you sometimes finish a piece of writing before it's really done? How do you react and what do you do when you are "told" to rewrite or revise?

Educating Others in the Ways of Collaborative Writing

- How would you explain collaborative writing to someone who has never written with someone else, someone who may think that writing with a coauthor is not nearly as valuable as writing alone?

A Final Opportunity for Trying Out Collaborative Writing

Collaborative Presentation

In order to find out more about how the discipline of Composition Studies forms a foundation for collaborative writing, team up with someone to do research about a topic, issue, theory, or scholar that you've been introduced to in this book. In order to reach agreement about the topic or related set of topics that you will study together, you might begin by making individual lists of the ideas you have read about in this book that you'd like to spend some time learning more about or investigating further. Share your lists with one another to see where they intersect. You may have to do this a few times—narrowing the shared list until you reach a single topic or set of topics.

Next, you and your co-writer will have to determine what the focus of your investigation is. What is it that you want to learn or know more about? This part of the collaborative process relies most on conversation with one another. Some writers accomplish this by creating a "title" for their work as a way to come to conceptual agreement; other writers generate questions back and forth until they reach the one that feels "right" to them both.

Once you have your focus or question, use the **Works Cited** and **For Further Reading** sections of the chapters to choose some relevant books or articles. You will have to determine whether you will both read all of the selections or how you will divide the work—and whichever way you do it, you will also have to determine how to share what you learn with one another and keep your reading/research focused on the question or concept you generated together.

As you proceed, keep in mind what you've read in the book about the importance of conversation and building on one another's ideas. Your goal will be to plan an oral presentation to be delivered jointly to your peers who, most likely, have not read the same materials. Rather than merely summarizing what you have read, you will be presenting the materials through the focus of the question or concept that you both agreed upon. It is this question or concept that will connect what will be new knowledge for your peers to the ideas about collaborative writing they have read in this book.

Index